Clear**Revise**®

OCR Cambridge National
Creative iMedia J834 (R093)

Exam tutor and practice

Published by
PG Online Limited
The Old Coach House
35 Main Road
Tolpuddle
Dorset
DT2 7EW
United Kingdom

sales@pgonline.co.uk
www.clearrevise.com
www.pgonline.co.uk
2023

PG ONLINE

ACKNOWLEDGMENTS

The questions in this textbook are the sole responsibility of the authors and have neither been provided nor approved by the examination board.

Every effort has been made to trace and acknowledge ownership of copyright. The publishers will be happy to make any future amendments with copyright owners that it has not been possible to contact. The publisher would like to thank the following companies and individuals who granted permission for the use of their images or content in this textbook.

Images: © Shutterstock
Ed's Dinner image page 22 © Pegasus Pics / Shutterstock.com
Chinese diner image page 22 © Alex Cimbal / Shutterstock.com
Mr Dz Route 66 Diner page 22 © image rawf8 / Shutterstock.com

Design and artwork: Mike Bloys / Jessica Webb / PG Online Ltd
Editor: James Franklin
First edition 2023. 10 9 8 7 6 5 4 3 2 1
A catalogue entry for this book is available from the British Library
ISBN: 978-1-910523-89-6
Copyright © PG Online 2023
All rights reserved

CONTENTS AND CHECKLIST

WHAT MAKES THIS GUIDE SPECIAL?

This guide is your personal exam tutor. It offers you a complete walk-through of the specification and related questions in a convenient format.

The best way to ace an exam is to practise... but that doesn't mean just endlessly doing past exam papers.

Imagine you were going to run a 100-metre race. If you really wanted to win it, you'd need a coach. They would analyse how you run and give you advice and lots of little improvements that you could make to win. Of course, you'd do some practice runs, but without coaching, you would have little idea how to improve.

Section 1

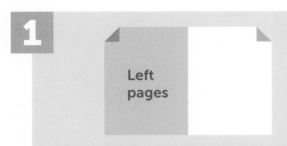

Study questions with model answers

Start on the **left-hand pages**. Left-hand pages coach you through each topic area on the specification. We show you some questions and model answers that would get full marks. We also give you exam tips on exactly what the examiner is looking for from the question or question type.

Apply your understanding to related topics

Now it is your turn! Once you have finished looking at the model answers on the left, **right-hand pages** provide you with a set of similar exam questions on the same topic. You should do really well in these as you've just seen model responses and tips on related questions.

Section 2

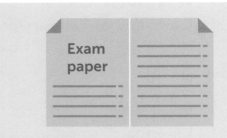

Complete a full practice exam paper

Now is your chance to have a go at a real exam paper. You need to attempt 70 marks in 90 minutes, so allow yourself around 1 mark per minute, plus 20 minutes at the end for improving any sketches, adding annotation to diagrams and correcting those silly mistakes we all tend to make.

When you take the paper, make sure you have a clear desk, turn off your phone and find somewhere quiet. Give yourself the same amount of time as a real exam.

Once you've completed each paper, the answers are in the back of the book for you to mark yourself. Good luck!

[1] ✓ Learn from the mark schemes

Mark your work using the mark scheme provided at the bottom of each page.

By the end of Section 1, you will have gone through lots of model answers and had a go at questions on every topic in the entire specification.

If you still feel that a topic needs more work, just use the smile icons ☺ or make a note on the page so that you can look up the topic later or ask your teacher for help.

THE SCIENCE OF REVISION

'Low stakes' examination practice

Practising past examination questions is a powerful way to revise and improve your understanding of the subject. Mark schemes and professional guidance provide valuable information too. Without the added pressure of the big day and the stressful atmosphere that an exam hall may create, studying all of this in a calm atmosphere where the results don't matter to anyone but yourself, creates the most effective environment for the retrieval of information.

Retrieval of information

Retrieval practice encourages students to come up with answers to questions.[1] The closer the question is to one you might see in a real examination, the better. Also, the closer the environment in which a student revises is to the 'examination environment', the better. Research shows that students who had a test 2–7 days away did 30% better using retrieval practice than students who simply read, or repeatedly reread material. Students who were expected to teach the content to someone else after their revision period did better still.[2] What was found to be most interesting in other studies is that students using retrieval methods and testing for revision were also more resilient to the introduction of stress.[3]

Feedback and note-taking

The tips and advice included with each model answer constructively focus purely on how to get more out of each question or type of question. Every topic shows model questions and answers, along with advice from experienced teachers and opportunities for students to try further similar questions. Answers and tips are displayed on the same page allowing for immediate feedback.[4] There is space for notes – use this if you need to. Making summarised points at the end of a revision session is the most effective way to use notes.[4]

Ebbinghaus' forgetting curve and spaced learning

Ebbinghaus' 140-year-old study examined the rate in which we forget things over time. The findings still hold true. However, the act of forgetting facts and techniques and relearning them is what cements things into the brain.[5] Spacing out revision is more effective than cramming – we know that, but students should also know that the space between revisiting material should vary depending on how far away the examination is. A cyclical approach is required. An examination 12 months away necessitates revisiting covered material about once a month. A test in 30 days should have topics revisited every 3 days – intervals of roughly a tenth of the time available.[6]

Summary

Students: the more tests and past questions you do, in an environment as close to examination conditions as possible, the better you are likely to perform on the day. If you prefer to listen to music while you revise, tunes without lyrics will be far less detrimental to your memory and retention. Silence is most effective.[5] If you choose to study with friends, choose carefully – effort is contagious.[7]

1. Roediger III, H. L., & Karpicke, J.D. (2006). Test-enhanced learning: Taking memory tests improves long-term retention. *Psychological Science*, 17(3), 249–255.

2. Nestojko, J., Bui, D., Kornell, N. & Bjork, E. (2014). Expecting to teach enhances learning and organisation of knowledge in free recall of text passages. *Memory and Cognition*, 42(7), 1038–1048.

3. Smith, A. M., Floerke, V. A., & Thomas, A. K. (2016) Retrieval practice protects memory against acute stress. *Science*, 354(6315), 1046–1048.

4. Kluger, A & DeNisi, A. (1996). The effects of feedback interventions on performance. Psychological bulletin, 119(2), 254–284.

5. Perham, N., & Currie, H. (2014). Does listening to preferred music improve comprehension performance? *Applied Cognitive Psychology*, 28(2), 279–284.

6. Cepeda, N. J., Vul, E., Rohrer, D., Wixted, J. T. & Pashler, H. (2008). Spacing effects in learning a temporal ridgeline of optimal retention. *Psychological Science*, 19(11), 1095–1102.

7. Busch, B. & Watson, E. (2019), *The Science of Learning*, 1st ed. Routledge.

HOW TO FIX MISTAKES IN YOUR EXAM

We all make mistakes, and the chances are that you'll make one or two in the exam.

If you realise that you've made a mistake in an answer, it's no problem.

Cross the answer out so that it is obvious that it's a mistake.

Example 1 – Put a line through the incorrect answer:

(c) A spy in a film hides around a corner out of breath. They are extremely worried.
Explain **one** camera angle or shot type that could be used for this shot.

~~An extreme wide shot would help to show the spy in their surroundings~~

An extreme close up of the eyes would help to show the fear in them.

Example 2 – Put a line through each incorrect word.

(c) A spy in a film hides around a corner out of breath. They are extremely worried.
Explain **one** camera angle or shot type that could be used for this shot.

A ~~long shot~~ extreme close up of the eyes would help to show the fear in them.

Example 3 – Put a cross through a section of writing.

(a) Describe how the lighting chosen for this scene could help to create a warm and friendly mise-en-scène.

~~The shot type that has been chosen allows for the main actors to be seen in the surroundings.~~

~~Extra cast is seen enjoying themselves in the background along with other props such as tables and~~

~~chairs add to the warm feel of the location.~~

They could choose to use lighting colours which have warm tones such as orange. The position of the

lighting highlights different areas of the scene and helps to create a happy atmosphere around

the main characters and other actors.

But DON'T scrub out answers:

(c) A spy in a film hides around a corner out of breath. They are extremely worried.
Explain **one** camera angle or shot type that could be used for this shot.

Exam tip

If you cross out an answer but don't write anything else, the examiner is allowed to mark it.

But they can't mark it if they can't read it because you scrubbed it out.

PAPER 1

CREATIVE iMEDIA IN THE MEDIA INDUSTRY

R093/01

Information about Paper 1

Written exam: 1 hour and 30 minutes

40% of the qualification

70 marks

All questions are mandatory.

Section A consists of 7-10 closed response, multiple choice and short answer questions. Questions will be chosen from across all topic areas.

Section B consists of a short scenario which will develop throughout the rest of the paper. Any type of question may be asked along with three extended response questions. Questions will be chosen from across all topic areas.

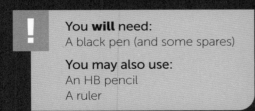

You will need:
A black pen (and some spares)

You may also use:
An HB pencil
A ruler

1.1   SECTORS IN THE INDUSTRY

Left pages contain example questions with model answers. The answers will get full marks.

① Start on the left hand page.

1   (a)   Identify **two** sectors of the traditional media industry.

1   *Print publishing*

2   *Film*

[2]

Exam tip

Identify questions ask for an answer from a number of possibilities. They require short answers.

Exam tip

There may be more than one answer that is correct.

In this case, **radio** and **television** are two other media sectors you need to know about in the **traditional media industry**.

The **new media** industry includes the sectors of **computer games**, **interactive media**, **internet** and **digital publishing**.

(b)   Which **one** the following is a product produced by the digital publishing sector of the media industry? Tick (✓) the correct box.

A   Special effects (SFX, VFX)   ☐

B   Music   ☐

C   eBooks   ✓

D   Video   ☐

[1]

Exam tip

Special effects (**SFX**) occur on set during filming, such as prosthetics and explosions. **Visual effects** (**VFX**) are computer generated, and added in post production.

Do you remember?

Give a list of products that the media industry creates.

- *Video*
- *Audio*
- *Animation*
- *Special effects (SFX, VFX)*
- *Digital imaging and graphics*
- *Social media platforms/apps*
- *Comics and graphic novels*
- *Digital games*
- *Websites*
- *Multimedia*
- *eBooks*
- *Augmented Reality (AR) / Virtual Reality (VR)*

③ Do you remember boxes often include revision questions to help you think about the topic. Cover the answer and try the question.

Exam tip

Multiple choice questions usually use the command word **Tick**. Make sure to only tick one box unless the question says otherwise.

④ Look at the right-hand page and have a go at some exam style questions on the same topic. The questions below are worth five marks, so you should be able to finish them in five minutes.

2 (a) Below are four sectors of the media industry. Which is a new media sector?
Tick (✔) the correct box.

A   Radio

B   Television

C   Film

D   Digital publishing

[1]

(b) Identify **two** other new media sectors that are not given in part (a).

1 ....

2 ....

[2]

3 An app is being built for a clothing shop.
Identify **two** media products that could be contained in the app.

1 ....

2 ....

[2]

⑤
Cover the answers with
a sheet of paper so that
you're not tempted to cheat!

⑦
Are you confident?
Fill in one of the faces to
show whether you feel you
did well in the topic or if
it needs more revision.

⑥
Mark yourself
Once you've finished the questions, mark them
using the answers at the bottom of the page.

Total

/ 5

☹ 😐 ☺

Answers

2 (a) **D** – Digital publishing [1].

(b) Computer games[1], interactive media[1], internet[1].

3 Images[1] (showing items of clothing), Video[1] (of models wearing the clothing), Graphics[1] (such as for icons or the interface), Animation[1] (such as for an animated logo or a button press).

1.2 JOB ROLES IN THE MEDIA INDUSTRY

1 Which role leads the creative decision making during all phases of the production of a film?
Tick (✓) the correct box.

   A Production manager

   B Editor

   C Audio technician

   D Director ✓

[1]

2 Active Immersion are producing a new computer game. Identify **one** role which will create the computer code for the game.

   Games programmer.

[1]

Exam tip

Explain questions need you to give a reason or a cause for something.

• The role

• The reason

Do you remember?

What are the **three** phases of production to create a media product?

Pre-production (before production), production, post-production (after production).

---

3 Explain the role of a copywriter in the production of a magazine advertisement.

   • *The copywriter will create the text for the campaign.*

   • *This will be written to entice or encourage the reader to purchase the product or service.*

[2]

Use any blank space to make notes.

Do you remember boxes may also contain other points on the specification which you need to revise before attempting the questions on the right.

Do you remember?

You need to be aware of the following roles in the media industry:

Creative roles: animator, content creator, copywriter, graphic designer, illustrator/graphic artist, photographer, scriptwriter, web designer.

Technical roles: camera operator, games programmer/developer, sound editor, audio technician, video editor, web developer.

Senior roles: campaign manager, creative director, director, editor, production manager.

4 A television drama called 'The Crucible' has been commissioned.

Write your mark here

(a) A camera operator is **one** technical role that will be required to film the drama in the production phase.

Identify **one** role that manipulates the video footage in the post-production phase.

....

[1]

(b) During the production phase the actor's speech will also need to be recorded.

Which of the following roles will be responsible for setting up microphones and other equipment to record this speech?

Tick (✓) the correct box.

A Sound editor ☐

B Production manager ☐

C Audio technician ☐

D Director ☐

[1]

(c) Once the drama is complete it will be advertised on billboard posters. A copywriter has already written the text for the advertisement.

Explain **one** role, other than copywriter, which will be involved in the creation of the billboard posters.

....

....

....

....

[2]

> **Exam tip**
>
> Explain questions normally give **two marks** for each point you make. If the exam has **three marks** for each point, then you need to give more detail.

Total

/ 4

☹ 😐 ☺

> **Answers**
>
> 4 (a) *Editor[1], video editor[1].*
>
> (b) **C** – *Audio technician[1].*
>
> (c) *A photographer[1] will take photographs of the actors[1].*
> *A graphic artist/illustrator[1] will create additional graphics/images required[1].*
> *A creative director[1] will lead the creative team[1] (graphic designers, illustrators, copywriters, photographers) and help shape the direction of the project/deliver the marketing strategy[1].*
> *Graphic designer[1] will create the overall layout of the billboard poster[1].*
> *Creative director[1] would be responsible making sure that the overall aesthetic / look and feel fits with the brand[1].*
> *Campaign manager[1] will be responsible for client liaison[1], organising tasks[1] and tracking project progress[1]. They may also allocate roles[1].*
> *Production manager[1] will manage the project/people/budget[1].*

2.1   STYLE, CONTENT AND LAYOUT

1   A magic show will be broadcast on television and also distributed via a streaming app.

(a)   Identify the purpose of the television programme.

To entertain the audience.

[1]

Do you remember?

What are **four** other purposes of media?

- *Advertise/promote*
- *Educate*
- *Inform*
- *Influence*

(b)   **Fig. 1** below shows a magazine advertisement for the television programme.

Fig. 1

(i)   Identify how the elements of the advertisement have been positioned.

They have all been horizontally aligned to the centre.

[1]

(ii)   In some magazines, the advertisement will appear in colour. Explain **one** colour choice that could be used in the poster.

The use of yellow and orange where the glow lines are between the hands would help to give the

feeling of magic.

[2]

Exam tip

Other colours could have been chosen here. What is important is that your choice and explanation match. For example, the glow lines could be purple and blue to imply electricity and energy.

Do you remember?

Remember that you also need to be aware of the following components of style, content and layout:

- Conventions of genre
- Formal/informal language
- Style of audio/visual representation
- Tone of language

2 A secondary school has introduced a new fruit salad option to its lunch menu.

Fig. 2 shows a poster that will be placed around the school building.

Tasty Fruit Salad

Our exquisite new fruit salad option is a delectable delight. Light and healthy, it's a great way to start your afternoon of study.

Included in the Meal Deal

Fig. 2

(a) Identify **one** purpose of the poster.

....

[1]

(b) Explain how the tone of language of the poster could be improved.

....

....

....

....

[2]

Total

/ 3

Answers

2 (a) *To advertise/promote[1] the fruit salad option.*
To inform[1] students of the new option.
To influence[1] students to choose the new option.

(b) *The tone of language used is currently very formal[1]. It could be made more informal / appropriate for a teenage audience[1]. For instance, "Check out the new fruit salad…"/"Start your day with a zing!…"[1].*
[1 mark for other specific examples that could be improved in the text].

2.2 2.3 CLIENT REQUIREMENTS AND AUDIENCE DEMOGRAPHICS

1 A DVD is going to be created for the film drama *'One day, I will'*.

Fig. 1 shows the client brief that the film production company has given to a design agency.

Client brief — One day, I will

Objective:

Produce a DVD cover for the film.

Audience:

The cover should appeal to adults aged 18-30.

> **Do you remember?**
>
> Client briefs are usually **formal** documents that are **negotiated** with a client. They result from **meetings** and **discussion** about a project which results in a company being **commissioned** to carry out some work.

Fig. 1

(a) Identify the type of product that the design agency needs to produce.

A DVD cover.

[1]

(b) Other than the audience and type of product, identify **two** other client requirements which would be useful to include on the client brief.

1 *The content required on the DVD cover.*

2 *The timescale for completing the project.*

[2]

> **Do you remember?**
>
> What other requirements are included in client briefs?
>
> - *Purpose*
> - *Client ethos*
> - *Genre*
> - *Style*
> - *Theme*

(c) Explain **one** way the target audience will influence the content of the DVD cover.

The content will need to appeal to adults aged 18-30. For example, it could use photos of actors that

appear in the film that are in this age group so it relates to the target audience.

[2]

> **Do you remember?**
>
> Remember that audiences may also be segmented by:
>
> - Gender
> - Occupation
> - Income
> - Education
> - Location
> - Interests
> - Lifestyle

2 Adventure World is a theme park that has just created a new white-knuckle rollercoaster which they hope will increase ticket sales to the park. They would like to commission their marketing company, MTP, to make their next video advertisement which will be shown as internet adverts. The advert should target people who might enjoy the thrill of a new rollercoaster at the theme park.

A client brief has not yet been completed as discussions between Adventure World and MTP are still happening.

Write your mark here

(a) Identify the type of product that will be produced.

....

[1]

(b) Identify the purpose of this product.

....

[1]

(c) Identify the target audience for the advertisement.

....

[1]

(d) Describe **one** way the target audience will influence the content of the advertisement.

....

....

....

....

[2]

(e) Identify **one** other category that audiences could be segmented by.

....

[1]

Total

/ 6

😟 😐 😊

Answers

2 (a) *A video advertisement.[1]*

(b) *To advertise/promote the new ride/theme park[1]. To influence people to go to the park[1].*

(c) *Those who are interested in rollercoasters / fast rides[1].*

(d) *The content could have fast paced cuts in the editing[1] which would help to give a sense of adrenaline[1].*
The content could have a sound track with a fast beat / heavy percussion[1] helping to give energy to the advert[1].
The content could show people enjoying the ride / being scared on the ride[1] which would encourage people to go and discover the thrills that Adventure World has to offer[1].
Accept other appropriate answers that would appeal to people interested in rollercoasters.

(e) *Age[1], gender[1], occupation[1], income[1], education[1], location[1], lifestyle[1].*

2.4 RESEARCH METHODS

1   A television documentary is being produced about wildlife in the UK.

Initial research for the documentary found that there are 628 species of birds in the UK.

(a) State the reason why this type of data is quantitative data.

It has an actual value (number).

[1]

Exam tip

State questions require short factual answers or the factors or features of something.

(b) Explain **one** other type of data.

Qualitative data is data which describes the characteristics of something. (For example, an interview with a child about their views of birds in their garden.)

[2]

(c) Which **one** the following methods is a primary research method?
Tick (✓) the correct box.

A   Television ☐

B   Interviews ✓

C   Internet sites ☐

D   Books, journals, magazines and newspapers ☐

[1]

(d) Describe how a focus group could be used by the production company when researching resident's views of urban foxes.

The production company would first find a representative set of people who are residents in urban areas. They would then have them in a room with a researcher or presenter who asks the group questions. The group then discuss their views about each topic. The focus group may be filmed for the production company to refer back to. They may also consider using this footage in the final programme.

[3]

Do you remember?

List the different primary research methods and secondary research sources.

Primary research methods	Secondary research methods
• Focus groups	• Books and journals
• Interviews	• Internet sites/research
• Online surveys	• Magazines and newspapers
	• Television

2 A magazine article is being written about the most popular clothing brands for teenagers. The magazine has created an online survey to gather data about teenagers' views.

(a) An online survey is a primary research method. Identify **two** other primary research methods.

1 ....

2 ....

[2]

(b) Describe how the magazine could carry out an online survey about the most popular clothing brands.

....

....

....

....

....

....

[3]

(c) The magazine article publishes the statistic that 4% of teenagers hadn't heard of any of the brands featured. A student makes use of this statistic in a report they are writing.

Which of the following best describes the student's research?

Tick (✓) the correct box.

A   They are using quantitative information from a secondary source. ☐

B   They are using qualitative information from a secondary source. ☐

C   They are using quantitative information from a primary source. ☐

D   They are using qualitative information from a primary source. ☐

[1]

Total

/ 6

☹ 😐 ☺

Answers

2 (a) *Focus groups[1], interviews[1], questionnaires[1].*

(b) *The magazine could select people who are part of the target group / teenagers[1]. They would then send them a link via an email / put a link to the survey on their website/app[1]. Participants would then answer questions given on a form[1] by selecting boxes / typing answers[1]. The results would then be calculated/analysed by the survey software/researcher[1].*

(c) **A** – *They are using quantitative information from a secondary source[1]. [4% is a numeric statistic (a quantity) so a quantitative statistic. The magazine is a secondary source for the student as they didn't conduct the original online survey.]*

2.5   MEDIA CODES

1   The final scene in a period drama shows a couple leaving a church having just got married. The bride is wearing a traditional white wedding dress. The shot changes to an aerial shot which zooms out to show a beautiful view of the couple at the church surrounded by all their friends and family. The text 'Some dreams come true.' appears in a traditional serif font.

(a) Identify a symbolic code, technical code and written code that has been used in this film.

Symbolic code   *The white wedding dress and a church are both symbols that are associated with weddings.*

Technical code   *Zooming out from a scene, especially when an aerial shot is used is a technical code which helps to suggest the end of a film.*

Written code   *The use of a traditional serif font is a written code which helps to place the drama in a time from the past.*

[3]

> **Do you remember?**
>
> What is the difference between a serif and sans-serif font?
>
> *Serif fonts have small lines or strokes on the beginnings and ends of letters.*
>
> *Sans-serif fonts do not have these (sans means 'without' in French).*
>
> Serif font   *Sans-serif font*

One scene in the film shows the main character peacefully reading a book as she sits alone in the grounds of a stately home shown in **Fig. 1**.

Fig. 1

(b) Explain **two** possible shot types that would be suitable for this scene.

1   *A close up of the character which helps to show her face and emotions as she is reading the book.*

2   *A wide shot of the character which establishes the character in the surroundings to show the viewer it is peaceful and grand.*

[4]

2 A computer game features Captain Jolly, a pirate. **Fig. 2** shows one scene from the game which is set in the 1700s.

In the scene, Jolly is seen relaxing on the beach of Lagoon Island. Slow pans and fades are used.

Fig. 2

Identify a symbolic code, technical code and written code that has been used in this shot.

Symbolic code ....

....

Technical code ....

....

Written code ....

....

[3]

Answers

2 **Symbolic code:** *A pirate's hat / earring are commonly used to suggest a typical pirate.*[1]
Palm trees help to suggest a desert island.[1]

Technical code: *The slow pans and fades help to give a relaxing feeling.*[1]

Written code: *The text Lagoon Island is written in an old fashioned font style (Old English), helping to give a feel of the 1700s.*[1]

2.5 CAMERA TECHNIQUES AND TRANSITIONS

1 A spy film has a scene where a spy is chased through central London. The director would like to use camera movement which helps to show the high intensity action in the scene.

(a) Identify **three** uses of camera movement that would be appropriate for this scene.

Camera movement 1 *Quick pans (moving the camera from left to right) to follow the spy as they run.*

Camera movement 2 *Use a track and dolly so that the camera moves alongside the spy as they run.*

Camera movement 3 *Zoom into the spy as they are running.*

[3]

(b) The spy hides around a corner out of breath. They are extremely worried about getting caught.
Explain **one** camera angle or shot type that could be used for this shot.

An extreme close up of the eyes would help to show the

fear in them.

[2]

(c) The spy continues to run.
Explain **one** type of transition which would be suitable.

A series of quick cuts would help to keep the energy and

pace in the scene.

[2]

Do you remember?

List at least **five** different shot types.

- *Close-up shot*
- *Extreme close-up shot*
- *Medium shot*
- *Long shot*
- *Extreme wide shot*
- *Low angle shot*
- *High angle shot*
- *Aerial shot*

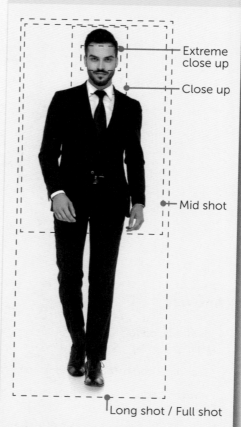

Extreme close up

Close up

Mid shot

Long shot / Full shot

Do you remember?

A cut is a transition which moves from one shot to another shot in one frame of video. What are **three** other transition types?

- *Fade (such as fade in, fade out, cross-fade)*
- *Dissolve*
- *Wipe*

There are also many other transitions available.

2 A television crime drama has a scene where a detective is starting to piece together all the different clues to a crime. The scene is fast paced to show them having a sudden realisation of what has happened. The scene shows lightning in a storm, a small chip in a car's paint work and a footprint.

(a) For each clue in the scene, explain a suitable shot type that could be used.

Lightning in a storm ....

....

Small chip in car's paint work ....

....

Footprint ....

....

[6]

(b) Describe **two** different ways in which camera movement could be used to keep the scene fast paced.

....

....

....

....

[2]

(c) Identify **one** transition that could be used between each shot.

....

[1]

Total

/ 9

☹ 😐 ☺

Answers

2 (a) *Lightning in a storm:* An extreme wide shot[1] to show the full extent of the storm / the drama of the lightning in the sky above the city [1].
Small chip in car's paint work: Extreme close up[1] so that the chip can clearly be seen[1].
Footprint: Close up[1] so that the full footprint can be seen[1]. Accept other suitable shot types with matching explanations that fit the scene.

(b) The camera could zoom into the lightning as it strikes[1].
The camera could be on a track and dolly and move along the car until it gets to the chip in the paint work[1]
The camera could tilt down to reveal the footprint[1].

(c) Cut[1]. Accept other transitions such as cross-fade/wipe/dissolve[1].

2.5 MISE-EN-SCÈNE

1   High Street is a soap opera which features people who live and work in the local area.

A scene is being filmed where a couple in the programme are out having a meal at a local restaurant.

A warm and friendly mise-en-scène has been created for this scene and is shown in **Fig. 1**.

Fig. 1

(a) Describe the features that make the scene warm and friendly.

They have chosen a location which has a traditional feel, with the use of wooden panelling

and soft furnishings. This helps to make it appear warm and homely.

The positioning of the main characters at the table helps to show them getting along and the other

characters are also positioned so they can be seen having friendly conversations.

The wardrobe chosen uses casual clothes which helps to give a relaxed atmosphere.

[6]

(b) Describe how the lighting chosen for this scene could help to create a warm and friendly mise-en-scène.

They could choose to use lighting colours which have a warm tone, such as orange.

The position of the lighting highlights different areas of the scene and

helps to create a happy atmosphere around the main characters

and other actors.

Natural light is coming in through the window and helping to lift the

amount of light in the scene. If there was not enough natural light,

a large light could be placed outside to simulate sunlight.

[6]

2 A TV thriller is currently in production. One scene, shown in **Fig. 2**, has a girl facing an area of a hospital where an unknown danger is lurking.

Fig. 2

(a) Describe how the mise-en-scène has been created to add tension to the scene.

....

....

....

....

....

....

....

[4]

(b) Explain how sound could increase the tension of the scene.

....

....

....

....

[2]

Total

/ 6

Answers

2 (a) *The location chosen has been stripped of any additional props/signage/furniture*[1] *so that the focus is on the character.*[1] *The composition of the shot focuses the eyes towards the girl*[1] *and then the light*[1]*. The light at the end of the corridor tells the viewer that something is ahead*[1] *and is the area to focus on.*[1] *The foreground is left dark as a contrast*[1]*. Wardrobe for the girl is simple*[1] *to create a clean silhouette.*[1]

(b) *The soundtrack could include low strings*[2] *which build in intensity/tone/crescendo*[1] [Note: Orchestral stringed instruments include *violins, cellos and double basses.]*

There could be a sound effect[1] *of echoing footsteps*[1]*.*
Accept other forms of audio which would help add tension to the scene.

3.1 WORKPLANS

1   A cover is being created for a fashion magazine. **Fig. 1** shows a workplan for the cover.

	Start	Duration	1	2	3	4	5	6	7	8	9	10	11	12	13	14	15	16	17	18	19	20
A																**Working Days**						
●Front cover																						
Photography	1	2																				
Page layout	3	2																				
Draft 1	5	2																				
Review	7	1																				
Draft 2	8	1																				
Final version	9	1																				
Back cover																						
Page layout	5	2																				
Advertising images	7	2																				
●Draft 1	9	2																				
Review	11	1																				
Draft 2	12	2																				
Print version complete	14	●1																				

C   B   D   E

Fig. 1

(a) Complete the table below to identify the different parts of the workplan.

Workplan part	Letter
Tasks	A
Timescales	B
Contingencies	E
Milestones	D
Activities	C

[5]

Exam tip

Milestones show a point in time of a major achievement in a project. They typically don't take time themselves to complete.

When using blocks in a workplan, an exam paper may show a period of time for an activity to be completed, at the end of which a milestone is achieved.

(b) Identify **one** item of hardware that may be involved in the basic retouching of the photograph.

A graphics tablet.

[1]

(c) Identify **one** job role that could be involved in the page layout.

A graphic designer.

[1]

Do you remember?

You need to be familiar with different resources that may be required for a project. These include:

• Hardware

• People

• Software

(d) Explain the purpose of a contingency with the use of an example.

This is a period of time at the end of a task or activity which is kept spare in case of any problems.

For instance, if a model for the photography could not attend the scheduled shoot due to another

project over-running, there would be two additional days for them to attend.

[2]

2   Predator is a company that has just created a new vacuum cleaner. They have commissioned an advertising agency to create a short video advert to be published on video streaming sites.

Predator already have video footage that they would like to be used as part of the advert.

Fig. 2 shows a workplan for the production of the online video advert.

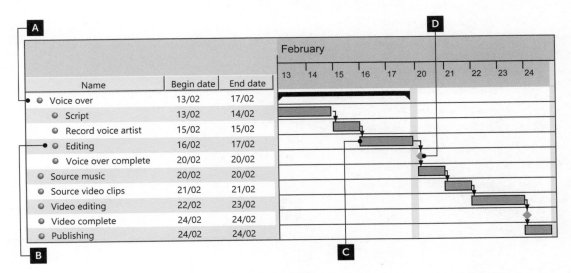

Fig. 2

(a) Complete the table below to identify the different parts of the workplan.

Workplan part	Letter
Tasks	
Timescales	
Milestones	
Activities	

[4]

(b) Explain **one** other item that could be included on a workplan.

....

....

....

....

[2]

Total

/ 6

😦 😐 🙂

Answers

2 (a)

Workplan part	Letter	
Tasks	A	[1]
Timescales	C	[1]
Milestones	D	[1]
Activities	B	[1]

(b) Contingency time[1] could be added to one or more activities/tasks which allows additional time in case of a problem occurring / task overrunning.[1]

3.2 MIND MAPS

1 BMX Extreme is a magazine for people interested in BMX racing, jumping and maintenance. The audience for the magazine has been identified as aged 12-24.

The magazine cover is going to be re-designed. **Fig. 1** below shows a mind map that has been created at the start of the planning process.

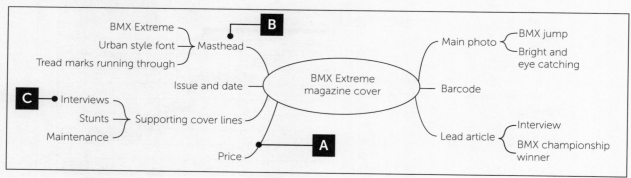

Fig. 1

(a) Identify the parts of the mind map labelled A, B and C.

A	Branch
B	Node
C	Sub-node

[3]

(b) State **one** purpose of a mind map when planning a magazine cover.

It helps to generate ideas for the content that needs to be included on

the magazine cover.

[1]

Exam tip

The question here is specific to the magazine cover, so make sure your answer is specific for magazine covers. A generic answer about the purpose of mind maps won't get the mark.

(c) Mind maps may be hand drawn. Identify **two** items of hardware that could be used to digitise a hand drawn mind map.

1 *Scanner*

2 *Digital camera*

[2]

Do you remember?

Other than ideas generation, what are some other purposes for mind maps?

- To show the content of a media product
- To show what resources/equipment will be needed to make a media product
- To show how different components of a media product relate to one another

2 BMX Extreme have decided to create an advertisement for the magazine which will be shown on television.

Write your mark here

As part of the pre-production planning, a mind map, shown in **Fig. 2**, has been created to show the resources and equipment required for the filming of the advertisement.

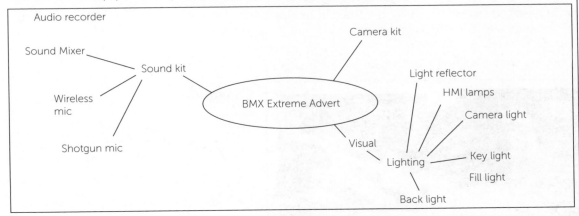

Fig. 2

(a) Other than resources and equipment, state **one** other purpose for which BMX Extreme could use a mind map.

....

....

[1]

(b) Identify **one** job role that may make use of the mind map.

....

....

[1]

(c) Identify **one** strength of the mind map shown in **Fig. 2**.

....

....

[1]

(d) Identify **one** weakness of the mind map shown in **Fig. 2**.

....

....

[1]

Total / 4

☹ 😐 ☺

Answers

2 (a) To help generate ideas for the video/advertisement.[1] To show the content of the video/advertisement.[1] To show how different components of the video/advertisement relate to one another.[1]

(b) A camera operator.[1] A director / director of photography.[1] An audio technician / sound engineer / sound mixer / boom operator.[1]

(c) It has a recognisable mind map structure[1] with nodes coming from the main idea[1] and branches to sub-nodes[1]. It has relevant equipment needed for the project[1].

(d) The 'fill light' sub-node doesn't link to lighting[1]. The 'audio recorder' sub-node doesn't link to the sound kit[1]. No equipment ideas/suggestions are given for the camera kit[1].

3.2   MOOD BOARDS

1   The Burger Pit is a restaurant based on the style of a 1950s American Diner. It serves both meat and vegetarian burgers, hot dogs, steaks, milkshakes and ice cream. They have just commissioned a company to produce their new website.

Fig. 1. Shows a pre-production mood board for The Burger Pit's new website.

Fig. 1

Discuss the suitability of the mood board in **Fig. 1** for the website design. You should include any areas for improvement.

The target audience for this mood board will be a web designer so that they are able to design and build the website, so I will discuss the suitability mainly from their perspective. I will also consider how suitable the mood board is for the client, who in this case is The Burger Pit.

A mood board should give a feeling of the potential style of a media product. The photos given here show the products that could be on offer to the customers and these have strong links to the style of a 1950s diner which is the style the client is looking to achieve. A website designer (or a graphic designer) will be able to pick out certain aspects, such as the car style or American flag style or colours for use in the website theme. Two different styles of photography are shown for the food: one is more rustic whilst the other is very clean and bright. These clearly help to show the products being sold. As two different styles are used, this is confusing for a designer. One style should be chosen so the designer gets the correct feeling from the mood board.

There are a number of items missing from the mood board. No examples of text and typography are shown and adding these would help the web designer when choosing particular font styles. Equally, no colour swatches or colour scheme is included, and adding this would help to see exactly which colours are most desired. No annotation has been used on the mood board. Annotation would help explain certain styles or features of the photos that could be focused on. Including textures of plastics or fabrics would also help when getting inspiration for the web design. In particular, there is no inclusion of styles for website menus, buttons or other GUI (Graphical User Interface) objects. Adding these would be very helpful to a web designer in understanding the desired look and feel.

[9]

| Suitability for the target audience | Strengths | Weakness | Suggested improvements |

Read this box before you have a go at question 2

2 Sunny Holidays are creating their new holiday brochure for families. The audience for the brochure is 20-45 year-old parents with children who are aged 1-15. As part of the pre-production planning, Sunny Holidays have created a mood board shown in **Fig. 2**.

Fig. 2

Discuss the suitability of the mood board in **Fig. 2** for the brochure design. You should include any areas for improvement.

....

....

....

....

....

....

....

....

....

....

....

....

....

....

Total

/ 9

[9]

Continue on a separate sheet if necessary   *See page 48 for how to mark your answer.*   ☹ 😐 ☺

Exam tip

For discuss questions make sure you show the following:

- A range of strengths
- A range of weaknesses
- A range of improvements

- Detailed knowledge and understanding of the suitability for the audience (in this case a web designer)

- Consistent use of appropriate terminology

Section 1   Creative iMedia in the media industry

3.3 VISUALISATION DIAGRAM

1 As part of the pre-production planning for The Burger Pit's new website, the web design company will create a visualisation diagram for the home page.

The home page will need to reflect the 1950s American Diner styles given in the mood board on **page 22**.

(a) Identify **one** purpose of the visualisation diagram.

It will show an outline of the home page in visual form.

[2]

Exam tip

The **visualisation diagram** here is being used to plan a web page. Giving generic answers about visualisation diagrams in general will not get any marks.

(b) Identify **one** user of the visualisation diagram and describe how they might use it.

A web designer could use the diagram to plan the layout of all the components of the web page.

[2]

Exam tip

There is **one mark** for the role and **one mark** for the description of how they might use the visualisation diagram. Other roles could be given, for example:

A web developer[1] could use the diagram to understand what program code they need to create[1].

A graphic designer[1] could use the diagram as a guide of the images and other graphics for GUI components that they need to create[1].

(c) Identify **three** items that could be included in the visualisation diagram.

1 *The Burger Pit's logo.*

2 *Images of the food or restaurant.*

3 *Annotation giving further details about components.*

[3]

Exam tip

Other items include:

• Title
• Colours
• Font styles
• Annotation

It is important to consider that the context is a web page, so you could include web page elements such as a navigation bar.

Do you remember?

If you are asked to create an improved visualisation diagram, what features do you think the examiner will be looking for?

• *Matches the scenario.*

• *Conventions are used.*

• *Relevant components (such as images, shapes, colours/colour scheme, font styles, font sizes, positioning/layout information).*

• *Annotation which justifies how improvements better meet the client's requirements.*

2 Big Outdoors is a book that has been written about fun outdoor activities such as building treehouses, tunnels or bonfires. It is aimed at adventurous children aged 11-15.

Fig. 1 shows a draft visualisation diagram for the book cover. The book cover will wrap around the front and back of the book. The book was written by Freya Walkingshaw and will be published by Adventure Press.

Fig. 1

Create an improved version of the draft visualisation diagram in **Fig. 1**. Marks will be awarded for:

• Relevant components and conventions used

• Layout

• Annotations that explain how the improvements better meet the client's requirements.

[9]

Total

/ 9

Use a separate sheet if necessary.

See pages 49–50 for how to mark your answer.

3.3 SCRIPTS

1 Pembury Zoo has commissioned a marketing company to produce a television advertisement to encourage more visitors to the zoo. The advertisement is aimed at families and promotes the many available attractions such as the assault course and water park. Part of the script is shown in **Fig. 1**.

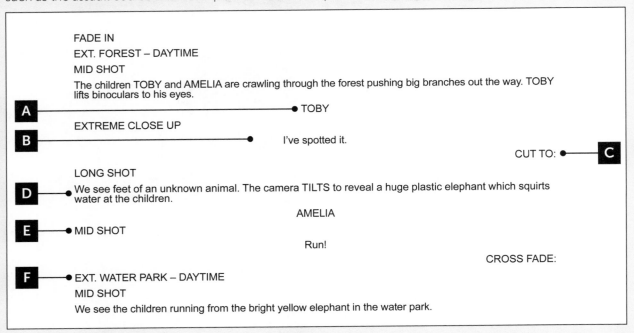

FADE IN

EXT. FOREST – DAYTIME

MID SHOT

The children TOBY and AMELIA are crawling through the forest pushing big branches out the way. TOBY lifts binoculars to his eyes.

A ──────────────────────────● TOBY

EXTREME CLOSE UP

B ──────────────● I've spotted it.

CUT TO: ●──**C**

LONG SHOT

D ●── We see feet of an unknown animal. The camera TILTS to reveal a huge plastic elephant which squirts water at the children.

AMELIA

E ●── MID SHOT

Run!

CROSS FADE:

F ●── EXT. WATER PARK – DAYTIME

MID SHOT

We see the children running from the bright yellow elephant in the water park.

Fig. 1

(a) Complete the table below to identify each of the script components in **Fig. 1**.

Script component	Letter
Shot description	D
Shot type	E
Transition type	C
Character name	A
Dialogue	B
Exterior location	F

[6]

(b) Explain **one** purpose of the script.

To give the lines of dialogue for each character so that the actors know what to say during the filming

of the advert.

[2]

Exam tip

Remember that the script will also be used to provide direction to the film crew.

2 FlameRock is a car tyre brand which has just created a new fuel-efficient tyre. They have commissioned their marketing company, MTP, to create a TV advert to promote the tyres. The script for the advert is shown in **Fig. 2**.

EXT. Car driving along a country road

EXTREME CLOSE UP of tyre slowly rotating showing the tread.

MALE VOICE-OVER (VO)

Some people love us for the grip.

Car quickly going around a bend on a hill near the sea.

MALE VOICE-OVER (VO)

Others love the noise.

Inside a car showing a family of two children and two adults on a trip. The soundtrack instantly goes SILENT to show how quiet the tyres are.

LONG SHOT the family has arrived at the seaside and have just started to eat ice cream.

MALE VOICE-OVER (VO)

But the new thing to love is the efficiency.

BOY AND GIRL

Thanks Dad.

Fig. 2

Explain **two** aspects of the script that require more detail, so that it becomes more useful as a pre-production document.

1 ....

....

....

....

2 ....

....

....

....

[4]

Answers

2 Some shots don't say which shot types[1] are needed. This means that the production crew/camera operator/ directory of photography won't know if the scene/equipment should be set up in a particular way[1].
None of the transitions are indicated[1] which means that a director hasn't been given a clear brief for the overall feel of the project. The director and editor may make their own interpretation of how the different shots should be edited together which isn't what the client is expecting.[1] No camera movements are indicated[1] so we don't know how the camera might pan/tilt in the different shots[1].

3.3 STORYBOARDS

1 A marketing company is currently in pre-production for a television advertisement showing all the different attractions in Pembury Zoo.

They have created a storyboard which is based on the script shown on **page 26**. The beginning of the storyboard is shown in **Fig. 1** below and will be given to the camera crew filming the advertisement.

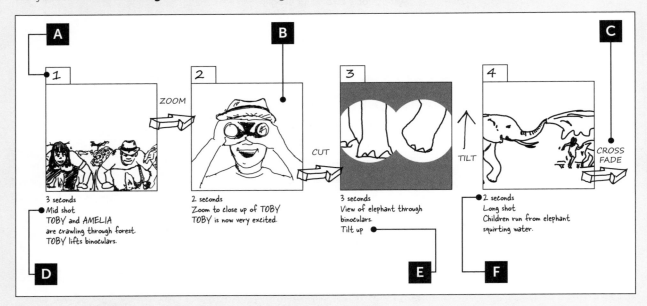

Fig. 1

(a) Complete the table below to identify each of the storyboard components in **Fig. 1**.

Storyboard component	Letter
Transition	C
Shot duration	F
Shot type	D
Shot number	A
Composition of scene	B
Camera movement	E

[6]

(b) Explain **two** reasons why a storyboard is a suitable planning document for the TV advert.

1 *It allows the director and film crew to see the sequence of the story and how the action flows from scene to scene.*

2 *It shows what components of each shot will be in view so that camera equipment and lighting can be set up before filming takes place.*

[4]

> **Exam tip**
>
> This question is asking about why a storyboard is a suitable planning document. You won't get any marks for giving components of a storyboard – the marks are for explaining why this is a suitable document.
>
> There are many other answers that could be given. For example:
>
> - It allows a **director** to make changes to shots/order easily in the planning stage, which reduces the need for costly changes if something doesn't work during production.
>
> - A **production manager** would use the storyboard to remind themselves of the actors, props and crew that are required for each day's filming.

2 A marketing company, MTP, is making the TV advert to promote FlameRock's new car tyres. The script for the advert is shown on **page 27**.

MTP has completed a storyboard for the TV advert which is shown in **Fig. 2** below.

Fig. 2

(a) Explain how camera movements shown in the storyboard will help the production team.

....

....

....

....

[2]

(b) Explain **one** aspect of the storyboard that requires more detail so that it becomes more useful as a pre-production document for production team.

....

....

....

....

[2]

Total

/ 4

Answers

2 (a) Production crew will position equipment[1] so that it doesn't appear in shot as the camera moves[1].
Lighting crew/technicians are able to see how the camera moves through the scene[1] so they can light it correctly[1].
Camera crew are able to choose the correct equipment[1] to create the necessary movement[1].
Film crew know where to place tripod/dolly tracks[1] to create the correct movement[1].
Director knows where to place the actors[1] so the camera can freely move around them[1].
Accept other suitable responses.

(b) Further information/clarity for each shot could be given[1] describing what the car/wheel/actors are doing[1] which would help the crew/actors understand what they need to do[1].
Timings could be added to the storyboard[1] which help the crew/director when filming / the editor when editing/cutting the video[1].
The addition of transitions[1] would help the editor when putting all the shots together / would help the crew understand how each shot will join together[1].

3.3 WIREFRAME LAYOUTS AND FLOW CHARTS

1 Abbie's Jewellery has commissioned JX Web Design to create the ordering page for their website. **Fig. 1** shows a wireframe for the basket page.

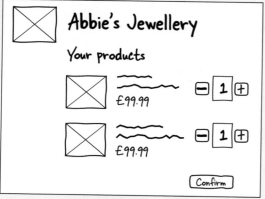

Fig. 1

> **Exam tip**
>
> The wireframe shows text that will be used. From the scenario this is a reasonable assumption of possible text. Annotation would be useful here to explain further.

(a) Describe the components that will be displayed for each item that is currently in the basket.

An image of the product will be shown on the left. The product name will then be shown above the price.

Two buttons will allow the user to increase or decrease the quantity of the product in the basket.

A text box will allow the user to enter an alternative quantity, as a number, for the product.

[4]

When the confirm button is pressed, the ordering process occurs as shown in the flow chart in **Fig. 2**.

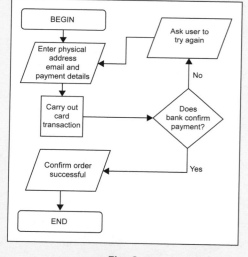

Fig. 2

> **Do you remember?**
>
> What are the common symbols used in flow diagrams?
>
>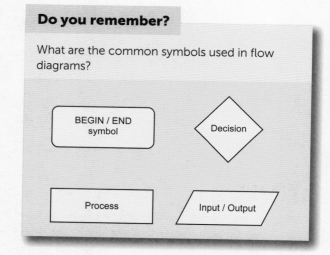

(b) Identify a user input, process and decision in the flow chart.

Input *Entering their physical address, email and payment details.*

Process *Processing the card details.*

Decision *Deciding what to do based on whether the bank confirms the payment or not.*

[3]

2 FlameRock have commissioned JX Web Design to make a new home page to help promote their new fuel-efficient car tyres. The site will feature their new TV advert. A wireframe of the homepage is shown in **Fig. 3**.

Fig. 3

(a) The company name and other title text is shown in the wireframe.
Explain **two** other components of the wireframe design.

1 ....

....

....

....

2 ....

....

....

....

[4]

(b) Draw **one** component onto **Fig. 3** that would allow the user to confirm they are happy to accept the Cookie Policy for the website.

[2]

Total

/ 6

☹ 😐 ☺

Answers

2 (a) *An image placeholder[1] is positioned top left to show where FlameRock's logo would be[1].*
A media player placeholder[1] shows the video advert should be in the centre.[1].
Text[1] is shown at the bottom to explain the cookie policy/terms[1].

(b)
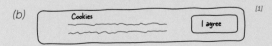
[1]

Allow alternative text for the button – e.g. 'Confirm', 'Agreed'.
Do not allow an × as this would close the pop-up but not ask the user to confirm their acceptance.

3.3   ASSET LOGS

1   A publisher is creating a book cover for a detective novel. The images that will be required have been stored in the asset log shown in **Fig. 1**.

Asset ID	Filename	Description	Properties	Source	Legal issues	Use
1	woman.eps	Female detective wearing coat (illustration)		Fresh Stock Image ref: 221862	Library – need to pay fee	Front of cover
2	leaves.jpg	Leaves falling		Mega Image Stock Image ref: 8591723	Library – need to pay fee	Front and back cover
3	footprint.svg	Illustration of black footprints		Internal design	Our copyright	Front cover
4	publisherlogo.svg	Standard publisher logo for back and spine		Internal publisher image	Our copyright	Spine and back cover

Fig. 1

(a)   Describe **two** technical properties that could be recorded in the properties column.

1   *The pixel dimensions of images could be recorded as the pixel width and pixel height.*

2   *The resolution of images could be recorded in dots per inch (DPI).*

[2]

> **Exam tip**
>
> **Properties** has been left empty here as question 1(a) is asking about them. An example of an entry in this column for pixel dimension and resolution could be:
>
> 1024 x 768 px
>
> 300 DPI

(b)   Explain why the source of an image would be useful to the book's graphic designer.

The graphic designer would be able to find the original high-quality image at the necessary resolution for use in the final print book cover.

[2]

(c)   Explain **one** reason why the description of an image will be useful to a graphic designer.

The particular image may be removed from the source website or image library. If the graphic designer has a description it will make it easier to find an alternative.

[2]

> **Exam tip**
>
> There are other reasons that the description could be useful. For instance, filenames are often not descriptive. If the image source and filename are simply a reference number then the wrong number could have been given. Adding a description allows the designer to check that the image they find is the correct one requested.

2 A web designer is creating a web page for a charity. They are creating a wireframe for the web page and are noting the assets the page will require.

(a) Three items which will be recorded in the asset log will be the asset ID, filename and image source.
State **two** other items of information that may be recorded in the asset log.

1 ....

....

2 ....

....

[2]

(b) Explain **one** detail that will need to be recorded when giving the source of any asset.

....

....

....

....

[2]

(c) Explain **one** reason why all assets need to be recorded in the asset log as soon as they are planned to be used in the website.

....

....

....

....

[2] Total

/ 6

☹ 😐 ☺

Answers

2 (a) *Image properties / image resolution / image dimensions / pixel dimensions [1], legal issues / copyright status / fees [1], use of the images[1]. [As this is a website, accept asset instead of image, or other types of asset such as video/audio.]*
[Do not accept asset ID, filename or image source as these are given in the question.]

(b) *The web address of the particular image[1] so that it can be downloaded[1].*
The name of the image library used and image ID number[1] so that it can be found/downloaded[1].
Record that the image is stored in a folder/library[1] which the web designer has on their computer/network[1].

(c) *A request for permission to use an asset may take time[1] so making the request earlier will help to prevent delays[1].*
If the web designer were to become ill/leave the company [1] then there would be a record of all the assets/ images required[1].
Another person could download the images/pay any fees/obtain the high quality version of the images[1] ready for when the web designer creates the web page.[1]

3.4.1
3.4.2
LEGAL ISSUES TO PROTECT INDIVIDUALS AND PROPERTY

1   JX web design has completed the ordering page for Abbie's Jewellery. A wireframe and flowchart for the website are shown on **page 30**. The information that is collected in the ordering process includes the customer's name, address, email address, credit card details and products ordered.

(a)   Abbie, who owns the business, is concerned about data protection.

   (i)   Identify **two** data protection considerations that must be taken when collecting data on the website.

   1   *Only collect the data that they need.*

   2   *Make sure that any pages that collect information, such as the ordering page, are secure.*

[2]

   (ii)   Identify **two** data protection considerations that must be taken when storing data on the website.

   1   *Store the data securely.*

   2   *Make sure the data is kept up to date.*

[2]

(b)   A customer posts on a review website giving Abbie's business one star and leaving the message:

"The product I bought was sold as 22 carat gold, but it doesn't have any gold in it."

The comment is false and Abbie is able to prove this.

Explain the legal issue for the person posting this comment.

This comment is defamatory as it affects the reputation of Abbie's business. Specifically, it is libellous as the comment has been published. Abbie would be able to sue the customer for any reputational damage caused.

[2]

Exam tip

Notice that this question is about collecting data. You won't get any marks by writing about storing data in answer to this question.

There are other considerations to make when collecting personal data such as:

- Only collecting data for the purpose given.

- Making the user aware of how their data will be used / asking them to agree to the terms and conditions (which include their data protection policy).

Exam tip

You also need to know what the implications could be if data isn't collected and held within the conditions of the data protection legislation. For instance:

- The business could be sued or prosecuted.

- A large fine could be issued.

Exam tip

Defamation is damaging a business or person's character or reputation with false information. There are two types of defamation:

- **Slander** is where the damaging statement is spoken and not published, such as a conversation in a restaurant.

- **Libel** is where the damaging statement is published, such as someone writing an article in a newspaper.

Do you remember?

What other legal issues do you need to know about the help to protect individuals and property?

- **Privacy rights** for recording and taking photos in public places or on private property.

- **Permissions** are needed to use images of photographs.

- **Harassment** and **invasion of privacy**.

- **Intellectual property rights** including copyright, patents, trademarks, creative commons licences, fair dealing, permissions, fees, licences, watermarks and symbols.

2   FlameRock have commissioned a new video advert of their fuel-efficient tyres. The video will be produced by the marketing company MTP. The script for the advert is shown on **page 27** and the storyboard for the advert is shown on **page 29**.

Write your mark here

(a) The FlameRock logo is used at the end of the advert.

Explain **one** symbol that should be placed next to the logo to help protect the intellectual property rights of FlameRock.

....

....

....

....

[2]

(b) One scene for the advertisement is of a family eating ice cream. MTP has found a suitable location.

Before MTP is able to film the scene, they must consider the permission and rights to use the location for filming.

Describe **one** legal consideration related to privacy that MTP will need to make before using the location.

....

....

....

....

[2]

Total

/ 4

☹ 😐 ☺

Answers

2 (a) *The trademark / TM symbol[1] should be placed next to the logo to show that it is a trademark[1] (and cannot be used by others to 'pass off' their products as made by FlameRock).*
The registered trademark / ® symbol[1] should be placed next to the logo to show that the trademark has been registered[1] (and has additional legal protections from being used without permission).
Remember that there are four symbols you should be aware of:
* *® – Registered trademark*
* *TM – Trademark*
* *© – Copyright*
* *㏄ – Creative Commons licence. [Creative Commons licences allow the free use of media assets. The licences may require you to acknowledge the creator of the assets (attribution), you may need to share your work with the same licence. Some Creative Commons licences may restrict use to non-commercial work only.]*

(b) *They will need to establish who the owner of the land/property that they wish to use is[1] as they will need to obtain permission[1] for filming commercially.*
They may need to also get permission from the owners of any buildings/houses/private property[1] that will appear in the background as they may also have rights to privacy[1].
Each of the actors involved would need to sign a model release form[1] which says that they allow MTP/ FlameRock to use their image for all the agreed purposes of their advertising[1].

3.4.3 REGULATION AND CERTIFICATION

1 (a) Complete the sentence.

An organisation responsible for regulation is the ASA.

ASA stands for *Advertising Standards Authority*

[1]

(b) State **one** other organisation responsible for regulation of the media industry.

Ofcom (The Office of Communications)

[1]

Exam tip

Complete the sentence questions are usually short recall questions worth one mark. They will often ask you to give the actual words that make up an acronym. For instance, they could ask for the meaning of HD in television resolutions (High Definition).

Do you remember?

What are the roles of the ASA and Ofcom?

ASA regulates advertising on TV, radio, billboards and magazines. They make sure that adverts conform to advertising codes. In particular they make sure that adverts are not misleading, harmful or offensive.

Ofcom regulates communication services such as television and radio. They investigate complaints from viewers or listeners and check if any of the Broadcasting Code rules have been broken. They make sure that programmes broadcast are not harmful or offensive.

2 A new film, based on a children's book, is aimed at young children aged 4-8.

(a) Identify the organisation which will be responsible for giving the film its certification.

BBFC (British Board of Film Classification).

[1]

(b) Explain an appropriate certificate which the production company will want to obtain for the film.

U (Universal). This type of certificate is suitable for all viewers, including children. Any higher certificates would be unsuitable for an audience of young children.

[2]

(c) The film has been very popular. As a result, a computer game has been released.

Identify the certification organisation which will issue a rating for the game.

PEGI (Pan European Game Information)

[1]

Do you remember?

What certificates are available for films and TV programmes

- **U** – Universal (suitable for all).
- **PG** – Parental Guidance (should only be watched by younger children if parents feel it is appropriate).
- **12A** – Suitable for 12+. Younger children may watch if they are accompanied by an adult.
- **12, 15, 18** – Suitable for 12+, 15+, 18+ year olds respectively.

Do you remember?

What PEGI age ratings are available for computer games?

- **3, 7, 12, 16, 18** – Each age rating shows the minimum age that the game is suitable for.

3 (a) Complete the sentence.

An organisation responsible for certifying computer games is PEGI.

PEGI stands for ....

[1]

(b) ASA is responsible for checking that adverts conform to advertising codes.

Tick (✔) the correct box.

A   Association for Standards in Advertising

B   Assessment Standards in Advertising

C   Advertising Standards Authority

D   Administration Standards Authority

[1]

(c) Explain the purpose of the BBFC.

....

....

....

....

[2]

(d) A news broadcast has upset a number of viewers.

Describe how Ofcom could become involved as a response to the complaints.

....

....

....

....

[2]

Total

/ 6

☹ 😐 ☺

Answers

3 (a) *Pan European Game Information.*[1]

(b) **C** – *Advertising Standards Authority.*[1]

(c) *The BBFC classifies films and TV programmes with an appropriate certificate*[1]. *These show which age range is appropriate*[1]. *This helps to make sure that people don't view inappropriate films*[1]. *[Note that BBFC classifies films and TV programmes that are shown in cinemas and released on DVD and Blu-ray. They do not classify TV programmes that are only released on broadcast TV.]*

(d) *Some of the viewers could complain to Ofcom*[1]. *This would result in Ofcom investigating the broadcast*[1]. *Ofcom would be checking to see that the broadcast was fair / gave both sides of the news item / wasn't harmful / wasn't offensive*[1]. *The broadcast would be checked against the Broadcasting Code*[1].

3.4.4 HEALTH AND SAFETY

1 Pembury Zoo are having a TV advert created. The script for the advert is shown on **page 26** and the storyboard is shown on **page 28**.

(a) For each of the aspects below, identify **one** health and safety risk and describe **one** method to reduce the risk.

Camera equipment *A track for a dolly camera will be a tripping hazard. If the dolly is on wheels, ensure the area is secured from the general public.*

Power cables *Power cables create a tripping hazard. They will need to be covered with mats and ramps to make them safe to walk over.*

[4]

Exam tip

There may be many different risks and ways to reduce risks.

For instance, a camera tripod will also cause a tripping hazard. Equally, an alternative way to reduce the risk of a track and dolly is to make sure that the risks are recognised and a skilled crew know how to reduce/minimise them.

Exam tip

Remember that the use of computers, in roles such as editing or visual effects in post-production, will also have health and safety risks to consider. For example, eye strain, neck and back problems.

(b) Before filming begins, a risk assessment will be completed.

Describe **one** purpose of the risk assessment for the filming of the TV advert.

It will identify all the safety issues that are associated with filming the TV advert in the zoo.

It will then show the measures that need to be put in place to reduce each of the risks.

[2]

Do you remember?

What is a location recce and why are they carried out?

*A **location recce** (short for reconnaissance) is where a number of the production crew visit the location that will be used for photography, filming or recording.*

They will decide which shots and action will work in the area.

They check the safety of the site, any permissions that may be needed, any sound or lighting issues (such as road noise or buildings that obscure sunlight at certain times of day).

They also check facilities such as toilets and parking areas.

Detailed notes and photographs will be made which will then help with deciding whether the location will be used. Recces will also be used in constructing an appropriate risk assessment.

2   Flamerock is a tyre brand that has commissioned MTP to create a TV advert for their latest fuel efficient tyres.

The script and storyboard for the advert are shown on **page 27** and **29**.

Two purposes of carrying out a location recce are to check for any hazards at the location and to determine if any lighting equipment will be needed.

(a)   Explain **two** other purposes of MTP carrying out a location recce for this TV advert.

1 ....

....

....

2 ....

....

....

....

[4]

(b)   The location recce has established that lighting equipment will be needed for the scene where the family is enjoying ice cream. A risk assessment will be carried out.

Identify **one** health and safety risk related to lighting equipment and describe **one** method to reduce the risk.

....

....

....

....

[2]

Total

/ 6

😞 😐 ☺

Answers

2 (a)   *To look at the location[1] and decide which shots/camera movement will work at the location[1].*
To check for any sound issues[1] such as background road noise[1].
To check the available facilities/toilets/parking areas[1] so that they are able to advise crew/actors where these are[1].
To check for power supply [1] in case equipment needs a power source[1].
Checking the best time to film[1] based on how busy it is[1].
Do not accept checking for any hazards / checking the safety of the area as this was excluded in the questions.
Do not accept determining which lighting equipment will be needed as this was excluded in the question.

(b)   *Lighting equipment could fall onto people[1] so lighting needs to be secured correctly[1].*
Power cables used create a tripping hazard[1] so these need to be covered so that people can safely walk over them[1].
Lights will get hot (if an indoors location is being used)[1] so sufficient ventilation is required[1].

4.1 DISTRIBUTION PLATFORMS

1 Power Systems is an electronics retailer with shops throughout the UK.

Every store has a 'Power Help' customer support area which helps customers to solve any problems they are having with their electronics.

They would like to improve the information that is available to customers whilst they wait for customer support.

They are considering whether to install a computer or kiosk to offer information.

(a) Explain **one** advantage and **one** disadvantage of using a kiosk rather than a computer.

Advantage *A kiosk is an enclosed system which means*

customers cannot connect/disconnect components such as the

display or keyboard. This helps to keep the system reliably running.

Disadvantage *If a change needs to be made to the kiosk, such as a*

larger touch screen, a new enclosure (or possibly an entirely new kiosk) would need to be purchased.

[4]

> **Do you remember?**
>
> **Kiosks** and **computers** are two **physical platforms** you need to know. What other platforms do you need to know about for the exam?
>
> - Interactive TV
> - Mobile devices

(b) A photographer wishes to share photos with a client.

Power Systems sell blank CDs and DVDs which are used for recording and the photographer is considering which of these to use.

(i) Identify the most appropriate format to use and explain your decision.

Chosen format *DVD.*

Explanation of your decision *DVDs store more data (8.5 GB on a double-layer, one-sided disc,*

compared to 650 MB for a CD). This means one disc will be able to backup more of the media files.

[3]

(i) Identify **one** other type of physical media that could be used to share the photos.

Memory stick.

[1]

> **Exam tip**
>
> The **physical media** types that you are meant to know for the exam are **CD**, **DVD**, **memory stick** and **paper-based** (for example, a physical print of a photo or a printed magazine).
>
> Be aware that **memory stick** is another name for USB flash drive.

> **Do you remember?**
>
> You also need to know about distribution online via **apps**, **multimedia** and the **web**.

2 A theme park takes photographs of its visitors on their rides which they offer for sale.

(a) Identify **one** physical media type which could be used to share a digital copy of the photo and explain **one** advantage of using this method.

Physical media type ....

Advantage ....

....

[2]

(b) The theme park will also be sharing the digital photos directly with visitors' mobile devices. Describe how this could be carried out.

....

....

....

....

[2]

Total

/ 4

😖 😐 ☺

Answers

2 (a) *A paper based / printed photo[1] as users are able to instantly see their photo / they don't need a computer or electronic device to view the photo[1].*
Memory stick/USB flash drive[1] are small[1] and easy to write information[1]. Most modern devices are able to read data from this type of device (as USB is commonly supported on digital TVs, computers, tablets and smartphones)[1].
Accept DVD/CD with an appropriate explanation (although these are less likely to be used today as many people don't have DVD/CD readers. Do not accept other non-physical methods of sharing the data (such as Bluetooth).

(b) *Bluetooth[1] could be used to share the photos. The user would pair/select their device with the theme park's computer[1]. The photo would then be transferred to their device for them to save in their photos/files/downloads folder[1].*
The mobile device could be connected using a cable[1] which connects to the USB port on the theme park's computer[1]. The photo would then be transferred to their device[1].
The theme park could ask the user to visit their website[1] and enter a unique code[1]. This would then allow them to view/download their photo[1].
The theme park could have an app that they ask users to download/install[1]. They could then have a unique code to enter / QR code that needs to be scanned[1] which then allows the photo to be viewed/downloaded[1].
The theme park could ask for their email address[1] and then email the files/photos to them[1].

4.2.1 4.2.4 IMAGE FILES AND COMPRESSION

1 A health magazine for teenagers has been created which will feature sports, active lifestyles and healthy eating.

(a) A photographer will take a photo of a model for the front cover of the magazine.

(i) Explain a suitable resolution for the photo.

A resolution of 300 DPI (Dots per Inch) is the standard for professional print publications so would be appropriate (as a minimum) for the photographs.

[2]

(ii) Identify the most suitable format for the image file to be saved as.

JPEG

[1]

(b) A web pop-up still advert is also going to be created. The advert will contain illustrated graphics and text.

Identify the most appropriate image format for the pop-up advert and explain why it is suitable for this use.

Image format   *PNG.*

Reason   *PNG works well with highly contrasting areas (such as black text and a white background). It is therefore more appropriate for images that will also contain text.*

[3]

Exam tip

Make sure to read the scenario and question closely as this could affect the possible suitable file formats. In this case, **JPEG** is the most acceptable format for storing photos out of the formats you are expected to know.

If an image needs to have transparency, then **PNG** should be chosen.

For vector images, **SVG** is usually a suitable choice.

Exam tip

The exam board will accept reasonable alternatives where they fit the question and scenario.

For this question you could have chosen SVG as the image format. The reason for using SVG is that it is a vector format, so text and the illustration would remain the same quality no matter what size they are displayed at.

Do you remember?

What is the purpose of compression and what do lossy and lossless compression mean?

Compression is used to reduce the size of a file. This will reduce the amount of storage space needed to store it and the time required to transfer it via the internet.

Lossy compression means that some of the original information is lost. Often when appropriate settings are used, the viewer or listener won't see or hear the difference.

Lossless compression means that none of the original data is lost. Once decompressed, the exact same data will be available.

2 A swimming pool has commissioned a graphic designer to create a three-fold printed leaflet to advertise their facilities and services.

(a) The graphic designer will be sourcing photographs and images to use in the leaflet.
Explain a suitable resolution for the designer to use.

....

....

....

....
[2]

(b) Explain a suitable format for the file that will be sent to the printers to create the final printed leaflet.

....

....

....

....
[2]

(c) The photos used on the leaflet make use of lossy compression.
Explain what lossy compression means in this context.

....

....

....

....
[2]

Total

/ 6

☹ 😐 🙂

Answers

2 (a) *300 DPI[1] as it has sufficient detail for printed products[1] and is the industry standard expected by professional printing companies[1].*

(b) *File format: PDF[1]*
Explanation: This file format is portable[1] and cross platform[1]. It is also the standard compatible file format that printers use[1]. It can contain a combination of text and images[1].
Accept TIFF[1] which is used for high resolution graphics[1] that can produce high quality prints[1].

(c) *Lossy compression means that some of the original information/data is lost in the compression process[1]. This will result in imperfections/detail being lost in the final image[1]. Lossy compression/compression results in a smaller file size than the original[1].*

4.2.2   AUDIO FILES

1   A software developer is creating an educational history app for children. The app contains background music, interviews and speeches.

(a)   The background music audio file will be compressed. Identify a suitable file format that could be used.

MP3

[1]

(b)   When exporting the final audio files to be used in the app, the software developer uses a bit depth of 16-bits and a sample rate of 44.1 kHz. Explain both these properties of audio files that have been used.

Bit depth   *This is the accuracy with which each sample is recorded. The higher the bit depth, the higher the quality of the audio.*

Sample rate   *This is the number of samples which are taken each second. In this case, 44,100 samples are taken each second. A higher sample rate will result in better quality audio.*

[4]

(c)   A famous speech is contained in the app. The software developer expects that children or teachers may want to hear the speech in the best sound quality possible.
Explain a suitable sound file format.

FLAC will keep all the original data for the speech as it is a lossless compression format, meaning that the sound quality will be exactly the same as the original audio.

[2]

Exam tip

The question hasn't asked for a compressed format, so a WAV file would also have been an appropriate answer. This format would keep the original data, but it would result in a larger file.

Exam tip

This question asks for a compressed format. MP3, AAC and FLAC would all be appropriate – however, MP3 is probably the most compatible of the three formats.

MP3 files use lossy compression which typically reduces the file size to 10% of its original size. It is widely used.

AAC is an alternative lossy compression with higher sound quality for the same bit rate and sample rate. It is again widely used.

FLAC is a lossless compression format. It typically reduces files to 50% of their original size. As it is a lossless compression, none of the original data is lost.

WAV is a format that has no compression. It will result in large file sizes, but there is no loss in quality.

2   A band is recording their new album at a recording studio. The sound engineer makes each recording at a bit depth of 24-bit and a sample rate of 96 kHz.

The final recording, which the public will listen to, will have a bit rate of 16-bit and a sample rate of 44.1 kHz.

(a) Explain why the sound engineer uses the alternative settings they have chosen.

....

....

....

....

....

....

[3]

(b) The recording studio wishes to release a compressed version of the music files to the public. Explain an appropriate file format to use.

....

....

....

....

[2]

Total

/ 5

Answers

2 (a) *The meaning of higher bit rate and higher sample rate must be given for 3 marks.*

A higher bit rate will allow for a greater accuracy/resolution to be recorded for each sample[1]. This will result in a higher quality audio file[1]. The higher bit rate will not clip very loud sounds[1]. Clipping is where a very loud sound is too big to be recorded. The sound is 'clipped' and leads to distortions or popping sounds for the listener. A higher sample rate will allow for more samples to be taken per second[1]. This will result in a higher quality audio file being recorded[1].

By using higher settings, the recording studio will have a higher quality version which they can release to listeners with higher quality equipment[1] / ensures the recording is suitable for any higher quality purposes in the future[1].

(b) *MP3[1] as it is a very common format for players to read / high level of compatibility[1].*
AAC[1] as it creates high quality files[1].
FLAC[1] as it uses a lossless compression which means all the original audio data will be retained[1].

4.2.3 MOVING IMAGE FILES

1   A film is being produced which will first be shown in cinemas and then be released on Blu-ray.

(a) Identify a suitable resolution for use in the cinema release.

4K

[1]

(b) Identify a suitable resolution for the Blu-ray release of the film.

HD

[1]

(c) The trailer for the film will be released via the internet. Explain a suitable file format for the trailer.

MP4. This format is compatible with most browsers.

[2]

(d) The film is shot at 24 fps. A particular scene will be slowed down. Explain why the original footage will need to be shot at a faster frame rate.

FPS means the number of frames that are recorded each second. A faster frame rate will be required

so that when it is slowed down (back to 24fps) the scene will appear in slow motion. (For instance, if

it is filmed at 120fps it will appear in slow motion when shown at 24fps.)

[2]

Do you remember?

What are all the resolutions that you should know for the exam?

- **8K** – *Some feature films and visual effects are shot at 8K.*
- **4K** – *Typical high-definition standard used in UK cinemas.*
- **4K UHD** – *(Ultra High Definition) Used on some more expensive Blu-ray discs and some for some streaming content.*
- **HD** / 1080p – *(High Definition) Used on standard Blu-ray, high definition broadcast TV and streaming platforms.*
- **SD** / 576p / 480p – *(Standard Definition) Used on DVD, broadcast TV and streaming platforms..*

Exam tip

HD (1080p) is one format that's suitable. **4K / UHD** Blu-rays need specialist players that support the format.

SD wouldn't be appropriate as the resolution is too low.

8K wouldn't be appropriate as most home TVs aren't capable of playing it and there isn't enough storage capacity on Blu-ray discs.

Do you remember?

What other video file formats are there?

All the following file formats use lossy compression unless otherwise stated.

- **MP2** / MPEG 2 – *For broadcast television, DVDs and some Blu-rays.*
- **MP4** – *For streaming video and some Blu-rays.*
- **MOV** – *Apple® format. Similar to MP4 in its capability, but less commonly used. May contain different formats.*
- **AVI** – *May contain compressed or uncompressed video. Suitable for high-quality video editing. Not suitable for streaming as reduced compatibility with devices.*
- **SVG** *is an animation format used on websites and banner adverts.*
- **GIF** *is an older format for animation which has been mostly replaced by SVG.*

2 A sports television programme is currently nearing the end of production.

(a) Explain a suitable resolution for the television programme to be broadcast at.

....

....

....

....

[2]

(b) Highlights of the sports programme are shown on the programme's website. Identify a suitable file format for the highlights video and explain why it would be suitable for its intended purpose.

Format ....

Reason ....

....

[2]

(c) A computer game related to the television programme has been created. Whilst the original television programme was filmed at a frame rate of 24 fps, the computer game will run at 60 fps.

Explain **one** advantage of using a faster frame rate.

....

....

....

....

[2]

Total

/ 6

☹ 😐 🙂

Answers

2 (a) SD / Standard Definition / 576p / 480p[1] as this is the standard for broadcast television programmes[1].
HD / 1080p / 1080i [1] as this is the high definition format for broadcast television programmes[1].
[Note: 1080p is progressive, each line of pixels is updated for every frame. UK TV often uses 1080i which means interlaced. Half the pixels are updated on one frame, then the other half of pixels are updated on the other frame.]

(b) MP4[1]. It can be viewed on a wide range of different devices / It is a compressed format which means the file size will be smaller / the use of a small file size will mean it will download/stream faster.[1]
Do not accept SVG or GIF as these are not suitable formats for video.

(c) The frame rate is the number of frames that are shown each second[1]. A faster frame rate will result in smoother motion[1]. This is suitable for sports/games which have fast motion[1].

From **3.2** Mood board on **page 23**.

Answers

How to mark your answer	Possible content you could include
Your answer should include similar points to those made on the right.	**Suitability for the target audience** • The target audience for the mood board would be a designer. • The mood board will also need to be suitable for the client – 'Sunny Holidays'.
Give your answer **7-9 marks** if it has the following features: • A **range** of strengths **and** weaknesses. • A **range** of suggested improvements. • A **clear explanation** of the suitability of the mood board for use by its target audience (the designer of the travel brochure and the client – NOT customers viewing the brochure). • **Consistently** uses appropriate terminology. • The discussion is **detailed** and **thorough**.	**Strengths** • Photos show people happy and enjoying their holiday. • Photos all show clear skies/good weather. • One photo shows the type of food available. • Most photos are of people within the target age.
Give your answer **4-6 marks** if it has the following features: • **Some** strengths **and/or** weaknesses. • **Some** suggested improvements. • **Sound** knowledge and understanding of the suitability of the mood board for a designer. • **Sometimes** uses appropriate terminology • An **adequate** discussion with **sound** understanding.	**Weaknesses** • One of the photos shows a couple that is outside of the age group given in the brief. • There aren't any examples of hotel facilities which could be featured. • There are no indications of colour swatches/colour scheme. • There is no annotation. • The font style would be more suited to adventurous travel and doesn't suit a family holiday.
Give your answer **1-3 marks** if it has the following features: • **Few** strengths or weaknesses are identified. • **Few** suggested improvements are identified. • Improvements are explained in a **limited** way. • **Limited** use of terminology. • A **brief** discussion with **limited** understanding.	**Improvements** • Change the photo of the older couple to one within the target age group. • Use a font more appropriate for a family holiday, such as a modern/clean/san-serif font. • Show a colour scheme/colour palette. • Show any textures that may be appropriate (such as palm tree leaves or sand).
Give your answer **0 marks** if you didn't attempt the question or it did not contain any points relevant to the question.	

From **3.3** Visualisation diagram on page on **page 25**.

Answers

How to mark your answer	Possible content you could include
Your answer should include similar points to those made on the right.	**Book layout** • The book cover shows the front and back pages. • The back page is on the left and the front page is on the right. • A spine is in the centre with text reading from top to bottom.
Give your answer **7-9 marks** if it has the following features: • A **comprehensive** document showing detailed understanding. • A **range** of suggested improvements are identified. • Improvements cover a **range** of components. • Conventions are **effectively** applied. • Justifications show **detailed** knowledge and understanding of the suitability of the document to meet the client's requirements.	**Relevance of content** • The format and styles used are suitable for the age group and outdoors topic. **Clarity of the idea** • The overall design works well together. **Components of the visualisation diagram** • Images. • Shapes. • Publisher logo. • Bar code.
Give your answer **4-6 marks** if it has the following features: • An **adequate** document which shows **sound** understanding. • **Some** suggested improvements are identified. • Improvements cover **some** components. • Conventions are **adequately** applied. • Justifications show **sound** knowledge and understanding of the suitability of the document to meet the client's requirements.	• Colours/colour scheme. • Font styles. • Font sizes. • Layout and positioning information. **Justifications for improvements** • Promotes the book.
Give your answer **1-3 marks** if it has the following features: • A **basic** document which shows **limited** understanding. • **Few** suggested improvements are identified. • Improvements cover **few** components. • Conventions are applied in a **limited** way. • Justifications show **limited** knowledge and understanding of the suitability of the document to meet the client's requirements.	• Informs the reader about the contents of the book. • Appearance of the cover. • Use of a house style for other books in a series. • Consideration of different distribution channels (ebook, physical book, images on a sales website).
Give your answer **0 marks** if you didn't attempt the question or it did not contain any points relevant to the question.	• Consideration of viewing devices/technologies (tablet, computer, epaper). • Accurate dimensions and layout.

From **3.3** Visualisation diagram on **page 25**.

For the marking grid for this question see the previous page.

This is one example of a visualisation diagram that could be created. Whilst you should try to draw neatly, you are not being assessed on your drawing abilities. You are being assessed on the ideas that you have given in your design along with the justifications of how your design improves on the original.

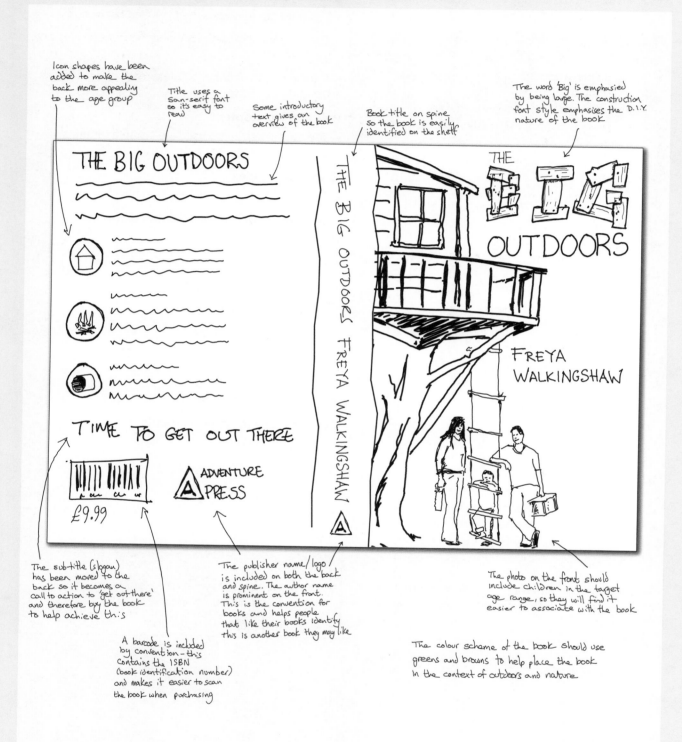

PRACTICE PAPER

Information about the practice paper

Before attempting the paper, go through the previous section of the book and revise any sections that you weren't confident about. Use the face icons at the end of each topic to reflect on your level of understanding and make your own judgement of what needs more revision.

Now to the paper.

Section A of the paper is worth 10 marks.

- These consist of 7-10 short answer, multiple-choice or close response questions.

- There will be at least one question related to each topic area on the specification.

Section B of the paper is worth 60 marks.

- A short scenario will be given which will develop throughout the rest of the paper.

- Questions will be closed response, short answer and three extended response questions.

- There will be at least one question related to each topic area on the specification.

You should do this paper under exam conditions.

Aim to make the desk you sit at look as similar to that in the exam room.

Turn off your mobile phone, music and remove all other distractions.

Let everyone in the house know that you can't be disturbed for 90 minutes whilst you do the paper.

You will need:

A black pen (and some spares)

HB pencil may be used for graphs and diagrams only.

Please write clearly, in BLOCK CAPITALS and black ink

Centre number .... Candidate number ....

First name(s) ....

Last name ....

Date attempted .... Time allowed: **1 hours 30 minutes**

LEVEL 1/2 CAMBRIDGE NATIONAL IN CREATIVE iMEDIA

R093/01 Creative iMedia in the media industry

PRACTICE PAPER

DO NOT USE
- A calculator.

INSTRUCTIONS
- Write in black ink
- Write your answer to each question in the space provided.
- Answer **all** the questions.

INFORMATION
- The total mark for this paper is **70**.
- The marks for each question are shown in brackets [ ].
- This paper has 12 pages.

ADVICE
- Read each question carefully before you start to answer.

Final mark .... / 70 = ... %

Section A

1 Identify **one** product produced by the print publishing sector.

....

[1]

2 Identify **one** job role that is responsible for creating the spoken dialogue used for a film.

....

[1]

3 The BBFC is responsible for rating films. What does BBFC stand for?
Tick (✓) the correct box.

A British Board of Film and Cinema ☐

B British Board of Film Certification ☐

C British Board of Film Censorship ☐

D British Board of Film Classification ☐

[1]

4 Identify **one** primary research method.

....

[1]

5 What is **one** purpose of a music track on a band's album?
Tick (✓) the correct box.

A To advertise ☐

B To educate ☐

C To entertain ☐

D To inform ☐

[1]

6 Identify **two** types of audio that are used to build suspense in films.

1 ....

2 ....

[2]

7 Complete the sentence.
In video resolution, UHD stands for:

U .... H .... D ....

[1]

8 A scene from a period drama is shown in **Fig. 1**.

Fig. 1

Identify **two** ways that help to create the mise-en-scène of the film scene.

1 ....

2 ....

[2]

Section B

The company myBand produce children's musical instruments aimed at 8 to 12-year-olds who would like to create electronic music.

The musical instruments include keyboards, drum machines and microphones for singers. Each one has built in music samples and accompaniments.

The latest kids' keyboard will be released by myBand in April next year. A promotional campaign for the new product will begin two months before release.

The new keyboard will feature more advanced sound effects, higher quality music samples and the ability to record and sequence music on an in-built display.

9   (a)   Identify **one** traditional media sector that could be used in the promotional campaign.

....
                                                                                                                    [1]

(b)   Identify **one** traditional media product that could be used to promote the new keyboard.

....
                                                                                                                    [1]

(c)   The target audience for myBand's musical toys is 8 to 12-year-olds who like music and technology.

(i)   Describe **one** way the target audience for the new keyboard will influence the content of myBand's promotional campaign.

....

....

....

....
                                                                                                                    [2]

(ii)   Before myBand starts creating any promotional media products, they would like to use a focus group to find out more about what current users think of their existing toys.

Describe how a focus group could gather or collect opinions about their existing toys.

....

....

....

....
                                                                                                                    [2]

10 **Fig. 2** shows a digital banner advert for the previous keyboard that myBand made.

Fig. 2

(a) Describe **one** way the graphic appeals to 8-12 year-olds.

....

....

[1]

(b) Describe **one** way the text has been formatted to emphasise some information.

....

....

[1]

(c) Describe **two** ways that the elements have been positioned to help promote the new keyboard.

1 ....

....

2 ....

....

[2]

(d) The digital banner advert needs to appeal to those wanting to play an electronic musical instrument.
     One way it does this is by showing a girl enjoying playing the keyboard.
     Explain **one** other use of graphics which will appeal to those wanting to play an electronic musical
     instrument.

....

....

....

....

[2]

(e) The banner advert will make use of animation.
Identify **one** other feature that a digital banner advert may make use of, which isn't possible in a print advert.

....
[1]

(f) Explain a suitable format for the banner advert to be exported as for use on a website.

....

....

....

....
[2]

(g) The top-right of the myBand logo contains the following symbol:

®

Explain the purpose of this symbol.

....

....

....

....
[2]

(h) Identify **one** organisation which will regulate the digital banner advert.

....

....
[1]

11   A new digital banner advert is being created which will feature a boy and girl playing the new digital keyboard.
     A photographer will take the photographs of the children in a dedicated photographic studio.

     (a) Describe **one** hazard that will need to be considered on a risk assessment.

     ....

     ....

     ....

     ....

                                                                                                                    [4]

     (b) One purpose of a risk assessment is to identify and record potential hazards.
          State **one** other purpose of the photographer carrying out a risk assessment.

     ....

     ....

                                                                                                                    [1]

     (c) The photographs taken will be used in both print and digital media adverts.
          Explain an appropriate resolution for the photographs.

     ....

     ....

     ....

     ....

                                                                                                                    [2]

     (d) The photographer collects the contact details of the parents and children at the photo shoot. Explain **one**
          way that the photographer must comply with data protection legislation when storing this data.

     ....

     ....

     ....

     ....

                                                                                                                    [2]

12 myBand will be creating a new web page as part of the promotional campaign for the new keyboard.

(a) Explain how a mood board will help when designing the website.

....

....

....

....

[2]

(b) Describe the roles of a web designer and web developer in the creation of the website.

....

....

....

....

....

....

....

....

....

....

....

....

[6]

13 The new keyboard that myBand is about to launch will contain music samples and accompaniments. The workplan for the creation of these is shown in **Fig. 3**.

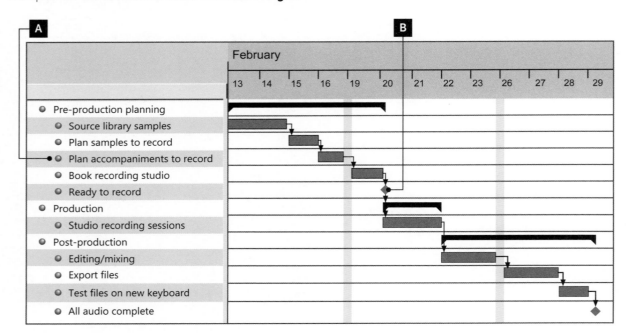

Fig. 3

(a) Identify the **two** parts of the workplan labelled A and B in **Fig. 3** by writing the label next to the correct description below.

Workplan part	Label
Timescale	
Task	
Milestone	
Resource	
Activity	

[2]

(b) The music samples and accompaniments that are created could be saved using lossy or lossless compression.

Explain the difference between lossy and lossless compression.

....

....

....

....

[2]

(c) Explain a suitable file format to store the music samples and accompaniments on the keyboard.

....

....

....

....

[2]

(d) The keyboard will allow users to save recordings from the keyboard. Identify a suitable form of physical media for saving the recordings so that they can be copied to other devices.

....

[1]

14 myBand will be creating a video advert to promote their new keyboard. The advert will be shown on video streaming sites and myBand's website.

Fig. 4 shows a draft storyboard that the camera operator will use when filming the TV advert.

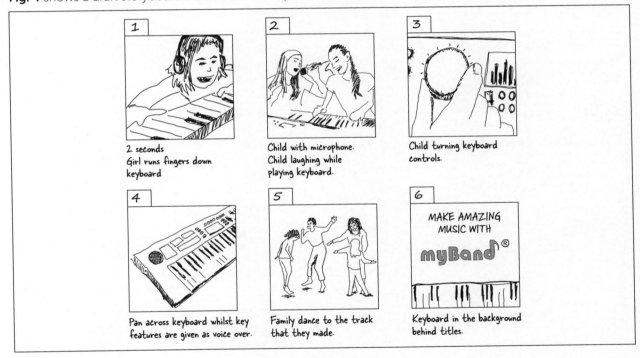

Fig. 4

Discuss the suitability of the storyboard for use by the camera operator.

Marks will be awarded for:

- Suggesting changes that improve the storyboard.
- Explaining how the changes you suggest will improve the effectiveness of the storyboard for the camera operator.

....

....

....

....

....

....

....

....

....

....

....

....

....

....

....

....

....

....

....

....

....

....

....

....

....

....

....

....

....

....

[9]

Continue on a separate sheet if necessary.

15 As part of myBand's marketing campaign they will also produce a post card which will be sent to music teachers, toy shops and members of the public on myBand's mailing list. The postcard will be used to promote the new keyboard.

Fig. 5 shows a draft visualisation diagram for the postcard. Note that the design is only for the front side of the postcard.

Fig. 5

Create an improved version of the visualisation diagram in **Fig. 5**.

Marks will be awarded for:

- Relevant components and conventions used

- Layout

- Annotations that explain how the improvements better meet myBand's requirements.

[9]

Continue on a separate sheet if necessary.

Now mark your paper and fill in your marks on **page 72**.

PRACTICE PAPERS ANSWERS
LEVEL 1/2 CAMBRIDGE NATIONAL IN CREATIVE iMEDIA

Section A

Question	Answer	Marks	Topic number
1	Books[1], posters[1], magazines[1], comics[1]. *Accept other common print publishing products. Do not accept ebooks.*	1	1.1
2	Scriptwriter[1].	1	1.2
3	**D** – British Board of Film Classification.[1]	1	3.4.3
4	Focus groups[1], interviews[1], online surveys[1], questionnaires[1].	1	2.4
5	**C** – To entertain[1]	1	2.1
6	Dialogue[1], soundtrack[1], silence[1], sound effects[1], vocal intonation[1].	2	2.5
7	Ultra High Definition.[1]	1	4.2.3
8	Lighting[1], composition[1] costume[1], production design / location[1], hair and makeup[1], props[1].	2	2.5

Section B

9

9 (a)	Film[1], Television[1], Radio[1], Print publishing[1].	1		1.1
9 (b)	TV advert[1], radio advert[1], billboard advert/poster[1], magazine advert[1]. *Accept other appropriate products that use traditional media.* *Do not accept products such as digital images, websites or social media posts as these are new media and the question asked for traditional media.*	1		
9 (c) (i)	A description for just one way from the following: • Content should be age relevant • Content should be relevant for the interests • Content should be relevant to lifestyle • Content should be relevant to parental income Example descriptions: • The content should appeal to children aged 8-12 years old.[1] One way to do this would be to show children from the age group playing with the new keyboard.[1] • The content should appeal to musical children.[1] It could show children making high quality music with the toys/keyboard.[1] *Accept other appropriate responses that describe how the campaign would fit one appropriate target audience.*	2		2.3
9 (c) (ii)	A group of people is chosen to represent the target audience[1]. One or more people from myBand (or a company commissioned to carry out the focus group) will lead the focus group[1]. They will then discuss with the group their thoughts/feelings towards the toys[1]. The session may be filmed / key points will be written down[1]	2		2.4

10

10 (a)	A girl within the target age of 8-12 years-old is shown playing the keyboard.[1] *Accept other explanations that are appealing to the age group.*	1		2.2
10 (b)	A larger font size is used for the slogan/main text, which helps draw the reader's eye to the text[1]. The key sentences have been formatted in bold which helps to emphasise them.[1] Capitalisation/capital letters has been used for 'NEW' which helps emphasise this feature.[1] Capitalisation has been used for 'BUY NOW' which encourages users to take this action.[1] Vertical lines help to separate each of the features of the piano.[1] The text contrasts well with the background making it easy to read.[1] *Accept other appropriate responses.*	1		2.5
10 (c)	The 'Buy Now' button is located in the bottom-right which is the conventional place you would expect to click a button.[1] There is white space left around the text/images which helps them to stand out.[1] There is space around the logo, which makes it clearly visible[1] and helps build brand recognition[1]. Key features are centre aligned/central to the advert making them easy to see.[1] *Accept other appropriate responses.*	2		2.1
10 (d)	The sound wave suggests music[1] which will be appealing to those who like music.[1] The sound wave looks technical[1] and will help entice those interested in the technical/electronic side of music making.[1] The logo makes use of a music note/quaver which helps to emphasise the musical theme.[1]	2		
10 (e)	Interactivity / the ability to click a button.[1] Audio/sound effects.[1]	1		2.5

10 (f)	SVG / Scalable Vector Graphics[1] as this is a common file format / compatible with most web browsers / as this allows for animation/interaction.[1] PNG[1] as this file format compresses well / has small file sizes.[1] *Allow JPG instead of PNG [but note that PNG is a better choice for images that contain text].* *Allow GIF for animation/common file format; however, do not allow interaction. Note that GIF is not as high quality as SVG so this may not receive marks if the question asked for the 'most' suitable filetype.* *Do not allow interaction for PNG, JPG or GIF as these formats do not have interactive capabilities.* *Do not allow animation for PNG or JPG as these formats do not have animation capabilities.*	2		4.2.1
10 (g)	The symbol indicates a registered trademark / registered trade mark[1]. This is used for logos/marks/symbols that are registered with the Intellectual Property Office / identify the owner of the goods.[1] It means that **myBand** can take legal action against anyone who uses the logo without permission.[1] *Do not accept just trademark as this has the symbol TM. Only give the first mark if 'registered trademark' is given.*	2		3.4.2
10 (h)	ASA / Advertising Standards Authority [1]. *Do not accept Ofcom / The Office of Communications as they regulate TV and radio programmes, not advertising.*	1		3.4.3

11

11 (a)	Lighting equipment[1] … …could fall on people[1] …could get hot[1] Power cables[1] … …could be a tripping hazards[1] Camera tripods[1] … …could be a tripping hazard[1] Wellbeing/safeguarding of children[1] …to prevent them from becoming fatigued[1] …to prevent them from becoming upset/hungry[1] *[Note that this risk is reduced by children having chaperones]* Risk of photographer falling[1] … …when standing on a ladder[1] Stands/background materials[1] … …falling on people[1] …trip hazard[1] *Accept other hazards that are appropriate to working in a photographic studio with child models.*	4		3.4.4
11 (b)	To record ways that the risks have been reduced / mitigated against.[1] To record the people who might be affected by risks.[1]	1		
11 (c)	300 dots per inch / 300 DPI / 300 pixels per inch / 300 PPI [1] …as this is the resolution required for printed products[1] (if digital products use a lower resolution the original photograph can be scaled down).	2		4.2.1
11 (d)	Only the contact details that are needed should be asked for[1] to help protect unnecessary personal data being processed/stored[1]. The photographer must give the parents/children the right to see their own data[1] and update their records if inaccurate[1]. The data should only be kept for as long as it is needed.[1] Once it is no longer required it should be securely destroyed.[1] The data should be stored securely using encryption/passwords.[1] Only authorised staff should be able to access the data[1].	2		3.4.1

12

12 (a)	Mood boards consist of a compilation of • Images/photos/illustrations [1] • Typography / font styles [1] • Textures [1] …which help to give the web designer/people creating the website an understanding of the feeling/style the website should have.[1] *1 mark for explaining what a mood board (for a web page) would contain.* *1 mark for explaining how it helps when designing the web page.*	2		1.4.3

12 (b)	**How to mark your answer**	**Possible factors and evidence you could use in your answer.** **You can use different ideas to these in your answer.**	6	1.2

Your answer should include similar points to those made on the right.

Give your answer **5-6 marks** if it has the following features:
- **Both** roles are described.
- Descriptions show **detailed** knowledge and understanding of the roles.
- How the roles help with the creation is **clearly** described.
- **Consistently** uses appropriate terminology.

Give your answer **3-4 marks** if it has the following features:
- Both roles contain description but may have an **uneven** balance between the description of each role.
- Description shows **sound** knowledge and understanding of the roles.
- How the roles help with the creation is **adequately** described.
- **Sometimes** uses appropriate terminology.

Give your answer **1-2 marks** if it has the following features:
- Description of at **least** one role is attempted.
- Description shows **limited** knowledge and understanding of the role.
- How the role(s) help with the creation is described in a **basic** way.
- Use of appropriate terminology is **limited**.

Give your answer **0 marks** if you didn't attempt the question or it did not contain any points relevant to the question.

For 3 marks or above it must be possible to see some differences in the two roles that show the web developer to be a technical role and the web designer role to be a creative role.

Web designer
- A creative role.
- Plans and creates the design and layout of the website.
- Creates design files in graphics editing software / Photoshop for layout of the web page.
- Converts design files into HTML and CSS.
- Work with graphic designers, content creators, copywriters and web developers.
- Reports to production manager or creative director.
- Tests their work to find problems/bugs and then fix them or report to appropriate people in their team.
- Makes use of any content management systems used by the company.

Web developer
- A technical role.
- Writes code for the web page.
- This may include front-end languages such as HTML, CSS and JavaScript.
- It may also include backend languages (such as PHP, SQL) on servers.
- Works with other programmers and web designers.
- Reports to a production manager.
- Creates and maintains documentation for any programming code they produce.
- Creates contingency plans for if the website goes down.
- Tests their work to find problems/bugs and then fix them.

Other points
- There is some overlap between these roles.
- For the creation of a small website, a single person, with the appropriate skillset, may carry out the work.
- The designer and developer may work together to test their work.

13

13 (a)	Activity **A** Milestone **B** *[note that tasks are the main parts of a project, in this case Pre-production planning, production and post-production.]*	2	3.1
13(b)	Lossy compression means that some of the original data will be lost[1]. Lossless compression means that all the original data will be kept in the compressed file[1] (once it has been decompressed).	2	4.2.4
13(c)	WAV[1] as it is uncompressed there will be no loss in quality / the keyboard is likely to have cheaper electronics so may not be able to uncompress the files[1]. MP3[1] as it is a compressed format, less storage space will be required[1]. *(If this were for a website or a download to a portable player, you would suggest MP3 as it is a common format with lots of compatible devices. In this case, the keyboard manufacturer would be able to specify the format, so it doesn't need to be a common format).* FLAC[1] it is uncompressed so files will have their original quality / it's an open/free format so a licence will not need to be purchased[1].	2	4.2.2
13(d)	Memory stick[1], USB removable storage[1], USB stick[1]. Acceptable other similar technologies such as SD Card. *Accept CD (although this would give an added expense to the keyboard and these formats are becoming uncommon).* *Do not accept DVD as this would require more expensive components and is more suited to video/film.*	1	4.1

14	How to mark your answer	Possible factors and evidence you could use in your answer. You can use different ideas to these in your answer.	9	3.3

Your answer should include similar points to those made on the right.

Give your answer **7-9 marks** if it has the following features:
- A **range** of strengths and weaknesses are identified.
- A **detailed** knowledge and understanding of the suitability of the storyboard for a camera operator (this is required to get marks in the top mark band).
- A **clear** explanation of how the effectiveness is improved.
- **Consistently** uses appropriate terminology

Give your answer **4-6 marks** if it has the following features:
- **Some** strengths and/or weaknesses are identified.
- Discussion shows **sound** knowledge and understanding of the suitability of the story board for a camera operator or other users/roles.
- **Some** suggested improvements are identified.
- **Sometimes** uses appropriate terminology.

Give your answer **1-3** marks if it has the following features:
- **Few** strengths or weaknesses are identified.
- Discussion shows **limited** knowledge and understanding of the suitability for users/roles.
- **Few** suggested improvements are identified.
- Where improvements are explained, this is done in a **limited** way.
- Use of appropriate terminology is **limited**.

Give your answer **0 marks** if you didn't attempt the question or it did not contain any points relevant to the question.

For 7 marks or above your answer must show the suitability for the target audience of a camera operator.

The question is asking for the suitability, so it needs you to give strengths and weaknesses for use by a camera operator. In addition, the question says that you should also suggest improvements and explain how they improve the effectiveness.

Remember, that this question is considering the storyboard for use by a camera operator. It is not asking you to improve the content/storyline of the advert.

Strengths
- The sketches are clear to see what angles and shot types are needed.
- The camera operator will understand how they need to set up their equipment from the sketches.
- Additional descriptions will help the camera operator to understand what action/expressions need to be captured from the actors/models.
- The amount of information given is consistent throughout (except for timings which is only given once).
- The panels appear to be in the order of the final advert.

Weaknesses, improvements and explanation of how they improve the effectiveness of the storyboard
- Timings are not consistent and not present on all shots.
- The fourth frame of the storyboard would especially benefit from timings as the camera operator needs to know how long the pan across the keyboard needs to take.
- Each shot should be numbered so that there is no ambiguity in the order. Crew can also reference a particular shot in discussions.
- None of the shots state the shot type/camera angle. Adding these would be useful to a camera operator in knowing which equipment/lenses to use.
- There is only one indications of camera movement. If these are required, the camera operator will need to know what they are. For instance, zooming in to the keyboard controls would help to show what is happening in context.
- The panning across the keyboard in the fourth frame could be indicated with an arrow on the sketch to help show the camera operator which direction they need to pan.
- The addition of transitions would help the camera operator to know if additional footage is required before or after the shot – for instance if it is needed for a cross fade.

15	How to mark your answer	Possible factors and evidence you could use in your answer. You can use different ideas to these in your answer.	9	3.3

	Your answer should include similar points to those made on the right.
	
	Give your answer **7-9 marks** if it has the following features:
	• A **comprehensive** visualisation diagram.
	• A **range** of suggested improvements are identified.
	• Improvements cover a **range** of components.
	• Conventions are **effectively** applied.
	• Justifications show **detailed** knowledge and understanding of the suitability of the document to meet the client's requirements.
	
	Give your answer **4-6 marks** if it has the following features:
	• An **adequate** visualisation diagram.
	• **Some** suggested improvements are identified.
	• Improvements cover **some** components.
	• Conventions are **adequately** applied.
	• Justifications show **sound** knowledge and understanding of the suitability of the document to meet the client's requirements.
	
	Give your answer **1-3** marks if it has the following features:
	• A **basic** visualisation diagram.
	• **Few** suggested improvements are identified.
	• Improvements cover **few** components.
	• Conventions are applied in a **limited** way.
	• Justifications show **limited** knowledge and understanding of the suitability of the document to meet the client's requirements.
	
	Give your answer **0 marks** if you didn't attempt the question or it did not contain any points relevant to the question.
		• Clarity of idea
		• Relevance of content (format, styles, suitability)
		• Components of visualisation used:
		  – Images
		  – Shapes
		  – Colours / colour scheme – by use of annotations / hatching / shading
		  – Font styles
		  – Font sizes
		  – Positioning / layout information
		  – Text – slogan, branding
		• Justifications for improvements e.g.
		  – Promotes the product
		  – Appearance of a postcard
		  – Use of a house style for company
		  – Consideration of the purpose of the postcard
		  – Consideration of the audience viewing the postcard		

The following shows a possible solution. Annotation on a visualisation diagram typically just describes information about the design. In this case the question has also asked for an explanation of how the improvements better meet myBand's requirements, so notice the additional explanations.

Alternative designs could include typical features such as a review or star rating from a magazine, newspaper or website.

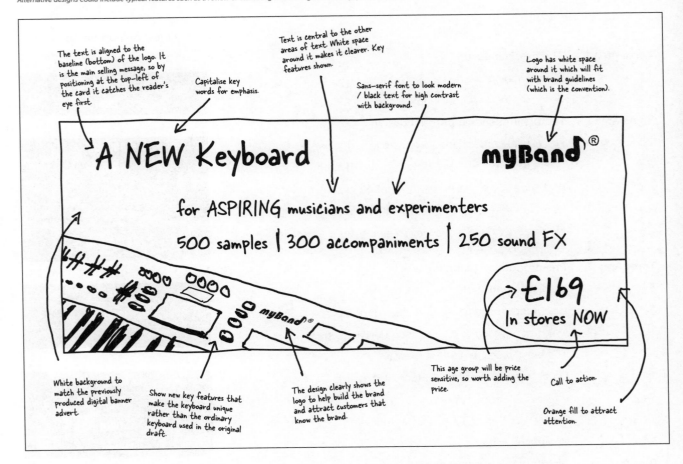

SPECIFICATION AND QUESTION MAP

Topic Area 1	The media industry	
1.1	Media industry sectors and products	1, 9(a,b)
1.2	Job roles in the media industry	2, 12(b)
Topic Area 2	**Factors influencing product design**	
2.1	How style, content and layout are linked to the purpose	5, 10(c-d)
2.2	Client requirements and how they are defined	10(a)
2.3	Audience demographics and segmentation	9(c)(i)
2.4	Research methods, sources and types of data	4,9(c)(ii)
2.5	Media codes used to convey meaning, create impact and/or engage audiences	6, 8, 10(b,e)
Topic Area 3	**Pre-production planning**	
3.1	Work planning	13(a)
3.2	Documents used to support ideas generation	12(a)
3.3	Documents used to design and plan media products	14,15
3.4	The legal issues that affect media	
3.4.1	Legal considerations to protect individuals	11(d)
3.4.2	Intellectual property rights	10(g)
3.4.3	Regulation, certification, and classification	3, 10(h)
3.4.4	Health and safety	11(a,b)
Topic Area 4	**Distribution considerations**	
4.1	Distribution platforms and media to reach audiences	13(d)
4.2	Properties and formats of media files	
4.2.1	Image files	10(f), 11(c)
4.2.2	Audio files	13(c)
4.2.3	Moving image files	7
4.2.4	File compression	13(b)

COMMAND WORDS

The OCR **command words** given below will be used in exam questions. They have been reproduced from the J834 specification with kind permission from OCR.

Command word	What you need to do
Analyse	Separate or break down information into parts and identify their characteristics or elements. • Explain the pros and cons of a topic or argument and make reasoned comments. • Explain the impacts of actions using a logical chain of reasoning.
Annotate	• Add information, for example, to a table, diagram or graph until it is final. • Add all the needed or appropriate parts.
Calculate	• Get a numerical answer showing how it has been worked out.
Choose	• Select an answer from options given.
Circle	• Select an answer from options given.
Compare and contrast	• Give an account of the similarities and differences between two or more items or situations.
Complete	• Add all the needed or appropriate parts. • Add information, for example, to a table, diagram or graph until it is final.
Create	• Produce a visual solution to a problem (for example: a mind map, flowchart or visualisation).
Describe	• Give an account including all the relevant characteristics, qualities or events. • Give a detailed account of.
Discuss	• Present, analyse and evaluate relevant points (for example, for/against an argument).
Draw	• Produce a picture or diagram.
Evaluate	• Make a reasoned qualitative judgement considering different factors and using available knowledge/experience.
Explain	• Give reasons for and/or causes of. • Use the words or phrases such as 'because', 'therefore' or 'this means that' in answers.
Fill in	• Add all the needed or appropriate parts. • Add information, for example, to a table, diagram or graph until it is final.
Identify	• Select an answer from options given. • Recognise, name or provide factors or features.
Justify	• Give good reasons for offering an opinion or reaching a conclusion.
Label	• Add information, for example, to a table, diagram or graph until it is final. • Add all the necessary or appropriate parts.
Outline	• Give a short account, summary or description.
State	• Give factors or features. • Give short, factual answers.

NOTES, DOODLES, GRADES AND DATES

....
....
....
....
....
....
....
....
....
....
....
....
....
....

Doodles

Grades

Target grade:

....

Practice paper mark:

.... / 70

Practice paper percentage:

.... %

Practice paper grade:

....

See page 73 for grade boundaries

Key dates

R093 exam:

....

R094 submission:

....

Optional unit submission:

....

EXAMINATION TIPS

With your examination practice, use a boundary approximation from the following table. Be aware that boundaries are usually a few percentage points either side of this.

Grade	Level 2				Level 1		
	Distinction*	Distinction	Merit	Pass	Distinction	Merit	Pass
Boundary	90%	80%	70%	60%	50%	40%	30%

1. Make sure your answers are given in the context of any scenario you are given.

2. Read questions carefully, you won't get any marks if you answer a different question that you think is being asked for.

3. When creating drawings such as a visualisation diagram, wireframe or storyboard, make sure you consider which job role(s) you are creating it for. For example, a visualisation diagram for a website homepage will require visual aspects along with annotation to explain the functionality and technical aspects.

4. Annotation of diagrams is important; for instance, adding notes about choices of font type, size and colour choices will be typical additions along with anything else relevant to the question.

5. You should include enough detail in your annotation so that a third party (such as a designer) could create the final product.

6. Don't focus on the quality of your drawing as much as the concept, annotation and explaining your choices.

7. If you use a pencil for sketches, make sure you press down to make clear marks. Light sketches won't scan well which will make it hard for the examiners to read.

8. Wherever possible, use the correct technical terms. For instance, saying that a shot type would 'show an actor's head full size on the screen' won't get the marks, whilst a 'close-up of the actor's head' will as it uses the correct technical term.

9. If you are given a discuss question, it often has a number of components that the examiner is looking for in your answer. For example, if you were asked to discuss the advantages and disadvantages of sharing photos on a CD or memory stick, you need to make sure your answer gives the advantages and disadvantages of using CDs and the advantages and disadvantages of using memory sticks. You could consider this question as having four sub-questions to it.

10. Do not give vague answers. For example, when describing hardware to produce an illustration, a 'tablet' won't get the marks. A 'graphics tablet' or 'tablet computer' would both be appropriate answers.

11. It's likely that you'll be asked to discuss or create an improvement of at least one of the following documents:

    a. Mind map

    b. Mood board

    c. Asset log

    d. Flow chart

    e. Script

    f. Storyboard

    g. Visualisation diagram

    h. Wireframe layout

    Make sure that you know the key components expected on each of them.

    Remember, annotation would be expected on all these documents except an asset log.

Good luck!

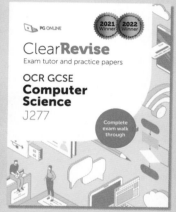
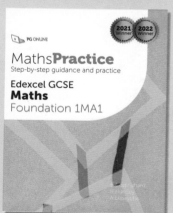

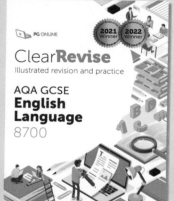
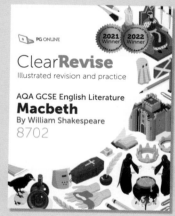
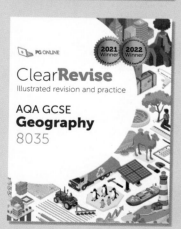

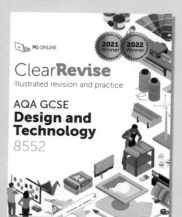
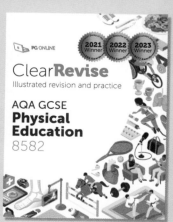